THE TIGER'S DESTINY

*Elusive when it needs to be, always unpredictable and majestic,
the tiger combines power and beauty in a way that few other
creatures can rival. No wonder it has affected man so deeply
since time immemorial.*

THE
TIGER'S DESTINY

VALMIK THAPAR

Photographs by
Fateh Singh Rathore and Mahipal Singh

KYLE CATHIE LTD

First published in Great Britain in 1992 by
Kyle Cathie Limited
7/8 Hatherley Street, London SWIP 2QT

Paperback edition 1994

Text copyright © 1992 by Valmik Thapar

Photographs copyright © 1992 by Fateh Singh Rathore and
Mahipal Singh, but see other acknowledgements on page 176.

ISBN 1 85626 142 5

A CIP catalogue record for this book is available from
the British Library

Designed by Clare Clements

Maps by Andrew Farmer

Typeset by Rowland Phototypesetting Ltd.
Bury St Edmunds, Suffolk

Printed and bound in Hong Kong
Produced by Mandarin Offset

For Paola,
without whose concern such a book
would have been impossible

and in the memory of Badhya,
whose sacrifice Ranthambhore
will never forget

*In the 1970s there was great concern all over the world about
decreasing tiger populations. More recently, the increased
visibility of the Ranthambhore tigers has made many people
think the problem is less severe than it is.*

CONTENTS

AUTHOR'S NOTE

This is the fourth book I have written concerning tigers and comes after sixteen years of active involvement with the area of Ranthambhore National Park. Because of my efforts to portray the many different aspects of the world of the tiger, it has become the most difficult book I have written and there are many people that I have to thank for it.

First of all I am indebted to a great library in the School of Oriental and African Studies, University of London, for providing me with a never-ending stream of information; and to the Victoria and Albert Museum, the British Natural History Museum, the Royal Anthropological Institute, AEDTA Paris, India International Centre, the French archives in Pondicherry and many wildlife and conservation organizations of the world.

I thank Peter and Sheila Lawton who housed me during my research in London; Romila Thapar for her patience in discussing the text with me; Fateh Singh Rathore and Mahipal Singh for their valuable and unique visual material; Gunter Zeisler and Tejbir Singh for providing me with some of their startling pictures; Sue Earle for her precious help in finding me material from the Far East; Pepita Seth for her lovely legend of Ayappa; Pupul Jayakar for her information on the Harappan seals; Shekhar Sharma for his recording of some of the beliefs of the people of Ranthambhore; the people of Ranthambhore for their patience in endless dialogue and discussion; P. C. Kunjumon for the hours spent on a computer; Sarah Butterworth for her help in gathering material; Tejbeer Singh Chowdhry for his support; and Caroline Taggart for all her enthusiasm and time in making this book work.

A special word of acknowledgement must go to Goverdhan Singh Rathore, without whose inspiration so little might have been possible in Ranthambhore.

Finally, there are no words to thank Paola Manfredi for her clarity and sharpness, and for the valid and incisive suggestions without which this manuscript would have suffered much.

INTRODUCTION

This is not just another book on tigers and their behaviour. It is an effort to encompass every aspect of the world of the tiger: the remarkable and powerful effect it has had on man; its fascinating natural history; and the magnitude of the problem that both the tiger and its habitat face in the immediate future.

The first section, 'The Cult of the Tiger', traces the distribution of the tiger from Siberia to Bali, exploring the numerous areas it has roamed in the past and the present. Wherever the tiger was found, it affected the life of forest communities and was absorbed into their cultures. Indeed, it seemed to create a link between nature and man throughout its range, from the frozen tundra of the north to the lush tropical forests of India. It played a major part in religion and ritual, as the protector of the people and the guardian of the forest. But when modern influences disrupted traditional ways of life, this connection between man and the tiger was severed. And there, it seems to me, lies the beginning of the problem.

A work of this kind can only touch the surface of this rich mine of information. Ranthambhore National Park represents a microcosm of the land of the tiger and I have drawn on my sixteen years' experience there to delve more deeply into the natural history of the tiger and its involvement with the needs of the people. The book now explodes into a visual section which conveys some of the reasons why this magnificent creature has inspired such respect and affection in man. Some of the pictures showing rarely photographed aspects of behaviour have been published before, but they are reproduced here in an attempt to provide a comprehensive portrait of the life of the tiger. I do not believe that a more fascinating range of tiger photographs has ever been published in one volume.

The final section of the book, 'The Tiger's Destiny', is an analysis of the problems of tiger conservation as they exist in Ranthambhore; they may be taken as representative of the problems which occur the world over. Protecting the tiger in isolation is not the answer: the tiger's future is interwoven with the problems of diminishing natural resources and increasing human demands. In fact, the tiger's destiny cannot be separated from the uncertain destiny of our planet.

Throughout my years in Ranthambhore I have been learning and relearning. This book is not intended to negate all that has happened in the past and that is happening at present. It is an attempt to understand a natural balance that has been upset, to share my own concern and to start to do something about a dangerous situation before it is too late.

Valmik Thapar
Ranthambhore, January 1992

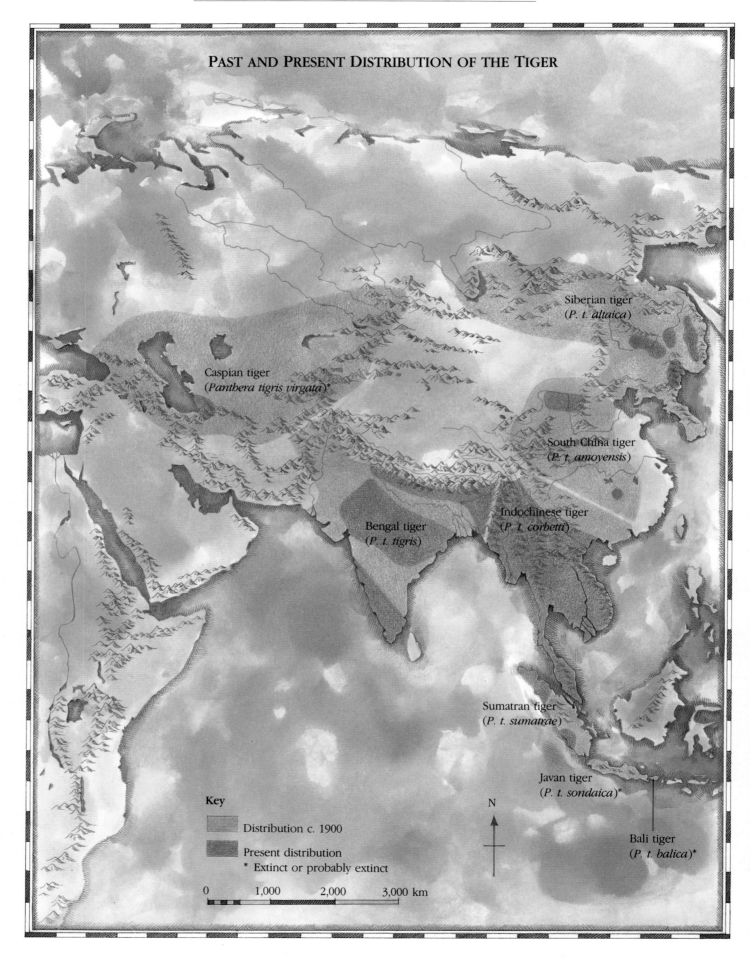

PAST AND PRESENT DISTRIBUTION OF THE TIGER

Siberian tiger
(*P. t. altaica*)

Caspian tiger
(*Panthera tigris virgata*)*

South China tiger
(*P. t. amoyensis*)

Indochinese tiger
(*P. t. corbetti*)

Bengal tiger
(*P. t. tigris*)

Sumatran tiger
(*P. t. sumatrae*)

Javan tiger
(*P. t. sondaica*)*

Bali tiger
(*P. t. balica*)*

Key

Distribution c. 1900

Present distribution

* Extinct or probably extinct

N

0   1,000   2,000   3,000 km

THE
CULT
OF THE
TIGER

*The image of the holy man and the tiger symbolizes the
close links the tiger had with all that was sacred. The calm
air of mutual acceptance between tiger and man
imparts a spiritual aura to the scene.*

Somewhere in Siberia millions of years ago a flow of molten lava from the depths of the earth formed the crater of what is now an extinct volcano. Slowly, over the centuries, it cracked and congealed to form a multitude of boulders. The area was cold, dark and inaccessible, and the first descriptions of it were written by travellers less than 200 years ago: 'Rugged mountain jaws opened upon us in all their grandeur. This was a terrific rent: the dark purple slaty rock had been riven asunder by granite and heaved up into craggy precipices of enormous height. In some parts the rocks were broken into sharp points; in others they were piled up like huge towers, overhanging the base of these mighty cliffs.

'Opposite one of the large islands are the high volcanic cliffs of San-doo; they jut far into the river and stand out of the water like gigantic castles, quite in keeping with the vast flood at their feet. Deep ravines have been cut in the mass by torrents which come tumbling down. They can only be heard, as groups of elm, ash and birch screen their falling streams, while the pine, aspen and other trees crown the summit.'

Once exploration became possible, a discovery was made in the heart of Siberia: it revealed the earliest known information on the origins of the tiger. Fossil records dating from the Pleistocene period were found deep within the Chigar caves of the New Siberian islands, indicating that a sabre-toothed tiger existed there millions of years ago. This tiger became extinct only about 10,000 years ago, and its descendants, the true tigers, began to extend their range, moving southwards in search of more suitable habitats as successive phases of the ice age made northern Asia uninhabitable.

Today, deep in the snows of the Soviet Far East, the Siberian tiger still roams. Its territory is a spectacular combination of plains and mountains, a coast facing the Sea of Japan and the River Amur flowing through startling landscapes. The plains of the Ussuri region stretch westwards, encompassing larch and dark conifer forests, and copses of dwarf pines peep from the summit of the mountains. Temperatures can sink as low as −35°C and the winters are bitterly cold.

But, alongside the tiger, man has managed to live in what must be some of the most hostile natural conditions in the world. Even at her harshest, nature allows those who can integrate into her patterns to survive. One early traveller was struck by the diversity of the region: 'Islands are frequent even here, where the stream is more confined and numbers of villages are found on both shores. The country is covered with forest as far as the eye can reach. Tigers and panthers are very numerous, and often visit the villages searching for prey.

'Nature has been exceedingly bountiful in this region, and has bestowed on the people some of her most valuable gifts. Magnificent forests contain timber suited for every purpose, oak for ship building, with elm, birch and pine for domestic purposes. She has stocked these vast forests with animals, many suited for the food of man, while others produce furs of great value, for which he can always find a market; and all multiply around him without giving him a moment's care.

'She has provided rich pastures for domestic animals and the luxuriant vegetation that springs up everywhere shows that man need only scatter the seed into the earth, to ensure an abundant harvest, while the Amoor and its affluents afford an inexhaustible supply of fish.'

On one of the rugged boulders on the bank of the Amur, archaeologists made an amazing discovery in the 1930s – the figure of a tiger, set deeply into one of the boulders, surrounded by other boulders bearing images of the elk, masked faces and clusters of writhing snakes. There are nearly 150 such boulders, and as the river rises and falls, the images appear and disappear. This ancient art is nearly as old as the Amur itself, and is almost certainly the oldest manmade representation of a tiger, dating back to 3500–4000 BC. It was the creation of the ancient tribes of the Amur, ancestors of the peoples who still share this land with the tiger.

One of these peoples, the Goldis, depended on fish for their survival, catching large quantities during the brief summer and drying them for use during the long, harsh winter. The dried fish was ground like flour into fish cakes called yukola, providing vital protein at a time when most other supplies were exhausted.

In this land of the tiger, little was wasted. The fishing nets were made from twine woven from the stalks of nettles which grew in abundance during the summer; the nets were boiled in reindeer blood to make them durable. The fish themselves were not only valuable as food: their skins were used to mend houses and to make clothing. Dried fish skin was crumpled into a ball by hand, rolled and pounded in a wooden mortar, then sewn together to make trousers or shoes, the latter with soles reinforced by reindeer hide. Men's clothing was normally made of salmon skin, while the women preferred fish with pretty stripes or bright colours.

Babies were placed in birch-bark cradles, padded with moss and shavings and suspended from the roof of the hut. Strings of the teeth and claws of various wild animals were dangled overhead to amuse the child, rattling as the cradle swung backwards and forwards. When an infant was a few months old it was given a fish's head on which to cut its teeth, and in a little while it was ready for its first suit of fish-skin clothes.

When entering the forest, the Goldis sought the favour of Anduri, the supreme god, and propitiated the forest god Kamtchanga with a gift of fish-meal cakes. The Europeans referred to them as 'fish-skin Tartars'.

The Goldis revered the tiger and the bear as their sacred ancestors. The tiger or *amba* was considered sacred as the guardian of the forest, and never hunted. It was the ruler or god of the wild regions. On the rare occasions when a tiger raided the hunters' snares for trapped deer, or carried off their dogs, or even ate the vital supplies of frozen fish that would see them through the lean periods, it was immediately forgiven. Anyone found killing a tiger was expelled from the tribe for having violated the traditions handed down by their forefathers.

Their religion was a mixture of totemism, nature worship and fetishism. The priests or shamans acted as intermediaries between the living and the supernatural world of the spirits. They had a diversity of duties – healing the sick, making sacrifices on occasions of misfortune or death, conducting prayers and even performing magic. They would bedeck themselves with fur robes, with the bones and teeth of sea animals and metal images of birds and beasts, making them look like a mixture of man and animal.

One shaman described how he was prompted into this service by a spirit who approached him in a dream: 'Sometimes she comes as a winged tiger. I mount her and she takes me to show me different countries. I have seen mountains where only old men and women live, and villages where you see nothing but young people, men and women. Sometimes these people are turned into tigers. Now my *ayami* does not come to me as frequently as before. She has given me three assistants – the *jarga* (panther), the *doonta* (bear) and the *amba* (tiger). They come to me in my dreams and appear whenever I summon them while shamaning.'

The invocation of the tiger spirit by the shaman was a vital facet in the religion of the Goldis. Ceremonial dress revealed their reverence for nature: elks, birds, the sun, tigers and snakes would be delicately embroidered into the branches of the 'tree of life' or 'tree of the world' – a symbol of that aspect of nature which was and still is the essence of all life.

An engraving of a tiger found on the rocks by the Amur river in Siberia. Dating back to 3500– 4000 BC, these are the oldest known manmade representations of the tiger.

Along with the early nineteenth-century travellers came other influences, seriously affecting the people's harmonious existence with the forest and the tiger. The natives of the land of the Amur fell victim to the harshness of Russian law and tax collection on the one hand, and Chinese liquor traders on the other. Both countries sent traders who bought animal skins and furs from the tribespeople for a tenth of their market value. At the same time, European hunters arrived, enticing the locals to act as guides and 'scent out' the animals in the primeval forests, especially the tiger. Demand for furs increased steadily and more and more animals were hunted each year. In the meantime, the introduction of alcohol had wrought its inevitable damage. As the people responded to the requirements of the intruders, their own religion, ritual and beliefs were sacrificed, their numbers declined and their way of life became harder and more impractical with each year that went by.

From those European hunters came the first records of the Amur or Siberian tiger: 'We thought (one of the guides) had found a herd, but on reaching him he pointed to the soft ground, covered with footprints and gore, where a terrible conflict had evidently taken place. At first we thought the boars had been fighting, but a closer inspection showed us that one had been measuring his strength with a more formidable foe – a tiger, whose footprints were stamped around the field of battle. The boar had been slain and carried off: it was easy to trace the crimson track, which led towards a mass of high reeds, into which the tiger had carried his prey. A well-trodden path of reedy tunnel formed the approach to his lair. The tiger had put down his burden at the entrance of this covered way, the red marks being distinctly visible. The men thought the battle had been fought three or four days ago; from this they concluded that a tigress and her cubs were in a den not far off; and in confirmation of their opinion, the dogs barked furiously.'

Even hunters armed with guns seem to have been awestruck at their first sight of a tiger: 'I felt an unbearable weight on my shoulders, as if someone was trying to push me into the earth,' one wrote. And indeed the Siberian tiger is one of the most remarkable subspecies in the world: it can weigh up to 350 kilogrammes and measure four metres from nose to tail tip, while its long warm coat and extra layer of fat protect it from the rigours of the harsh forests and deep snows. It hunts wolves and will snatch dogs from hunting lodges or villages. Some say it has been known to tear a horse from its harness and carry it off into the forest.

But deer and wild boar are the tiger's favourite prey. Residents of the coniferous taiga forests call the Siberian tiger the 'hog herdsman' because of the way it rounds up and chases a group of boar until it isolates a young hog to kill. Old boars with their formidable tusks are seldom threatened.

There are few recorded cases of the Amur tiger attacking or eating people except when cornered by hunters. But the hunters took their toll: by the middle of this century there were only about a hundred Siberian tigers left in the wild. Today there may be 200, and a single tiger has been known to range over an area of up to 150 square kilometres. Because of the harshness of their territory, little is known of their natural history and very few photographs exist.

As the tiger population decreased, so the religion of the Amur, in which the tiger figured prominently, faded. Now only a few people of the older generation retain the beliefs that integrated man, tiger and forest. Their traditions have been completely disrupted by the advent of 'modern civilization'. The future for these peoples and their culture is bleak. As we shall see, it is but one example of a once harmonious relationship between man and nature that we might do well to reconsider.

INTO THE CASPIAN

A princess waits on the bank of a river, desperate to cross to the other side. The waters of the river rage in front of her. Suddenly, a tiger appears by her side. She climbs on his back and they set forth to cross the waters. The tiger is a powerful swimmer and carries the princess safely to the other side. The princess gives birth to a baby on the far bank. The river is called Tigris and weaves a long course through the land, symbolizing the 'fertile connection' between man and the tiger in the legends of the area.

Early Sufism – the branch of Islam which is prevalent around the Caspian – encompassed a variety of existing doctrines and adopted the image of the tiger in carpets and textiles. It is apparent from these just how deeply the tiger was venerated – it is always depicted as the central figure, surrounded by a variety of other sacred objects. We shall see later that Islam also embraced the concept of the sanctity of the tiger in Indonesia.

Sadly, the last credible record of the Caspian tiger's existence in the wild was in 1958 and it is now almost certainly extinct. It used to live in the lowland forests and marshes bordering the Caspian Sea, but this area has now been converted into agricultural land. The local communities always held that the tiger harmed no one and there seems to have been a peaceful co-existence between man and animal. However, with much of its habitat destroyed, the tiger would have been forced to retreat to the mountainous regions and it slowly vanished, hunted out even from

Working drawings for panels used for decoration in Persia in the nineteenth century. The animals shown, notably the strangely maned tigers, were the most commonly used in Persia at that time.

these last refuges. At one time its range probably extended eastwards into Afghanistan and Pakistan, where its strongholds were the riverine forests along the Indus, but the last tiger in Pakistan is reckoned to have been shot at the turn of the century.

INTO KOREA

The Siberian tiger slipped into Korea through Khabarovsk, at the far eastern end of its range, where it was still found in the early years of this century. In Korea the tiger was a symbol of strength and courage. European travellers found it exceedingly difficult to gather information from the forest communities, who would deny all knowledge once they discovered that the visitors were looking for tigers. One hunter wrote, 'In vain did we offer, at length, extravagant prices for the beasts. Even fifty dollars, with the bones and carcass thrown in, for each tiger we shot, would not tempt them. . . . Although the people at Pochon strenuously denied the death of anyone there from tigers, and even the very existence of these beasts, yet Mr Campbell, when he visited that village in 1889, was told that in the last year eighteen people had been killed by them.'

The forest communities were guarding their deep-rooted links with the tiger, protecting it as best they could against the pressures of the hunters. But they were unable to hold out for long.

Many Koreans still believe that their land is blessed by the Blue Dragon and the White Tiger. Paintings of these creatures used to be a part of most Korean homes, supposed to repel evil spirits and protect the fortunes and destinies of the people. Much of this art has now been wiped out in the home, but it still exists in museums and temples. One of the finest examples can be seen in the Hwa Jang Sa temple in Seoul – it is a painting of a 'wicked woodcutter being eaten by a tiger in hell', and shows the vital role the tiger played as guardian of the forest.

Tiger skins were highly prized in Korea for the magical properties that enabled them to ward off evil; tradition also dictated that a tiger skin be draped over the bride's palanquin during a wedding procession, in order that the marriage be happy and produce many children. Nowadays, when there are probably no tigers in the wild in Korea, a thick cloth painted with stripes may still keep evil influences away.

The Koreans also venerated the tiger as the benevolent messenger of the mountain spirit San Shin, the most popular of their deities. San Shin is depicted as an old man with a white beard; he often holds a walking staff and a fan and is seated under a pine tree, accompanied by his messenger, the tiger. His popularity was so great that Korean Buddhism was forced to embrace him, and nearly ever Buddhist temple in Korea has a side shrine dedicated to San Shin.

Throughout Korea, the native people believe that the tiger is a protective figure, watching over the land. But for many years the country was dominated by the Chinese or the Japanese, both of whom exacted tributes paid partly in tiger skins. Combined with the damage wrought by hunting and deforestation, this means that the Korean tiger is almost certainly extinct.

INTO MANCHURIA AND CHINA

The Siberian tiger seems to have moved southwards into Manchuria, where it flourished a few hundred years ago in the northern and eastern part of the province, near the west bank of the Ussuri river.

Towards the end of the last century, the local people made yearly tributes of animals and furs to the emperor. Tigers were caught in large traps using pigs as bait. In one customs return dated 1896, tiger skins were listed at £6 each, though larger, well-marked skins could fetch as much as £15. The Manchurian tiger skin was considered much finer than the Indian. However, the European hunters met the same unhelpful attitude that they had found in Korea: 'The Chinese in the district said that there were tigers, but refused absolutely to lead me to their haunts, so greatly did they fear this animal,' wrote one. But he was misinterpreting the motives of the Chinese, who were not acting out of fear: on the contrary, they were protecting a vital and sacred element of their traditional beliefs.

Despite these efforts, hunting came close to wiping out the Manchurian tiger by the middle of this century. In 1980, the Quixinglazi nature reserve was created to protect the estimated fifty tigers surviving in the area. The reserve is covered with ancient forest through which run raging rivers. Nearby, on the Korean border, is the

A tiger screen, designed to protect the home and keep evil spirits away. It comes from Korea and shows how deeply rooted in Korean tradition the tiger was.

White Head mountain with its crater 'lake of heaven'. The mountain is considered sacred and monsters are believed to dwell in the lake in much the same way as in Loch Ness.

The tiger shares the area with snow leopards, sables, bears and the traditional forest people, the Oroquen. They are said to number 4,000 and live in tents of birch bark in the summer and deer skin in the winter. They hunt and raise reindeer and earn their livelihood from selling the deer's embryo, antlers, penis and tail, all of which are vital ingredients in Chinese medicine. They believe in spirits and shamans, especially in the fact that a shaman turns into a tiger after death.

The concept of were-tigers exists here. People believe that men can take the form of tigers and tigers can take the form of men. But both tigers and forest have been depleted and the traditional culture of these people is in conflict with the world around them.

China itself has been the home of four distinct subspecies of tiger: the most ancient tiger-like skull found anywhere was discovered here and estimated to be over two million years old.

This is a land of extremes, with the south-eastern islands enjoying a warm climate capable of producing tropical fruits while the north-east and parts of Tibet are perpetually ice-bound. Some of the world's highest mountains, deepest valleys and longest rivers are found in China: deserts, dark pine forest and tropical rain forests create a startling diversity of flora. Names given to places and buildings are revealing – black dragon pond, great wild goose pagoda, rock of granted grace, spring of the running tiger, temple of six banyan trees. . . . The list goes on and on and evokes a land and people inextricably intertwined with nature.

Even today, some Chinese people worship their ancestors and offer sacrifices of food to their deities. Early religions focused their worship on natural forces.

The Yunnan province in south-western China is a remarkable area where the average altitude is over 2,000 metres and the landscape is unspoiled. Here, between mountain passes, wild streams and tumbling waterfalls, live the Naxi peoples. They practise Bon, the pre-Buddhist religion of Tibet, and one of the features of their shamanism is the invocation of the tiger as a spirit. Tigers also figure largely on their ancient scroll painting. The Naxis created a written language over a thousand years ago using an extraordinary system of pictographs – their sacred text runs to 500 volumes! A line from this text says, 'When the sky and the earth were not yet separated, trees could walk and stones could speak' – summarizing the important role nature plays in their beliefs.

Among the Ch'uan Miao people, diseases and many other disasters were thought to be caused by demons and could be cured by exorcism. The belief that men could turn into tigers – and a variety of other creatures – and that tigers could turn into men was common. It was possible to turn into an 'evil tiger', but deceased fathers could turn into 'good tigers' to help their sons. A village would also have a *bontsong* or witch who could bewitch people and change them into tigers.

As one explorer wrote in 1912, 'Just as the dragon is chief of all aquatic creatures, so is the tiger lord of land animals. These two share the position of prime importance in the mysterious pseudo-science called *feng-shui*. . . . The tiger symbolizes military prowess. It is an object of special terror to demons and is therefore painted on walls to scare malignant spirits away from the neighbourhood of houses and temples.'

Another early traveller made similar observations: 'Then to a larger temple, gaudily decorated and in good repair, with a life-sized tiger (image) in a pen and in a

small "joss-house" of its own on the left of the entrance.
Propitiating this dreadful being by gifts of incense and
the regulation *kotow*, the pilgrims hope to secure themselves and their community from his depredations.' He
was not to know that this 'dreadful being' was in fact
the guardian and god of all the forest peoples.

The white tiger, found in India and then crossbred in
captivity all over the world, was an integral part of
Chinese ritual and belief and must once have been a
reality in their forests. The white image was regarded
as particularly sacred. Figures of white tigers feature in
many Chinese temples because of the belief that it was
the god of the west and controlled the wind and the
water: that is why the symbol of the tiger is placed on
the western side of some Chinese graves.

Since the earliest times, the tiger was associated with
animism and the worship of stars and animals. Its cult
was widespread among nomadic and pastoral peoples
and early hunters. The white tiger, Pai Hu, represented
the west and the autumn. It signified a season of storms,
believed to be caused by another tiger growling and

A tiger, crouched alert with its tail towards the sky, guards the entrance of the Fu Long temple in Dujiangyan, Sichuan, China, keeping away evil influences.

snarling, on the rampage for a mate. At this time the tiger was seen as the reincarnation
of the star Alpha, and lived like a tiger star in the 'silver stream of heaven' which we
know as the Milky Way.

For the tiger, Hu, to integrate into the Milky Way, he had to live for 500 years,
becoming Pai Hu or White Tiger, who would attain immortality in a further thousand
years when, as king of all quadrupeds, he could inhabit the moon or the silver stream
of heaven under the name of Pai Chon Chang. From here he protected planet earth.

According to the *I Ching* or *Book of Changes*, the book of divination which is
fundamental to much of Chinese philosophy, the universe reflects two contrasting
but complementary forces of energy known as yin and yang. These represent the
contrast between positive and negative, masculine and feminine, light and dark, and
are often symbolized as wind and water or as tiger and dragon. In the first serious
academic consideration of this belief, a paper by Bernhard Karlgren published in the
1930s discussed the strong possibility of the tiger being a fertility symbol, a 'yin'
animal full of the dark feminine force, and the idea has remained firmly established
ever since.

Taoism believes everything has a soul, be it animate or inanimate. When it is good,
it is controlled by yang or the green dragon; when evil by yin or the white tiger. The
breath of the tiger creates the wind, the breath of the dragon the clouds, and together
they produce torrents of rain which regenerate the earth and provide vital food for
man. In times of severe drought, real tiger bones would be dropped into a 'dragon
well', apparently causing such havoc for the reigning dragon that a vast storm would
engulf the land, bringing endless rain and relieving the drought.

The founder of Taoism, Chang Tao-Ling, was dedicated to the search for a dragon-
tiger elixir which would grant eternal life. After a thousand days of discipline and
instruction from a goddess, he was able to fight the king of the demons, to divide
mountains and seas and to command the wind and the thunder. The demons fled
and Chang Tao-Ling was able to ascend to heaven. His recipe for immortality is secret
and exists only in a few mysterious writings. But it is significant that Chang is always

depicted riding a tiger. Only in conjunction with the tiger could he fight evil and find the essence of eternal life. As we shall see, the tiger plays a comparable role in Hinduism as the vehicle of the goddess Durga.

A variety of objects bearing the image of the tiger have survived from the sixth and seventh centuries BC. Chains, cases and boxes of gold decorated with tigers evoke vast, dark forests where fierce struggles were a fact of life: battles between animals were reproduced on ornaments. It is obvious that an intense feeling of religious awe accompanied the sighting of a wild tiger.

The use of the tiger's image to ward off evil has lasted for thousands of years. In early times, Chinese soldiers wore imitation tiger skins with tails to guard against death in battle. A bronze cheekpiece in the shape of a tiger's head hung from a helmet and also protected the wearer in combat. Early ceremonial vessels were decorated with a tiger's or dragon's head with a serpent's tail curling behind. Chinese paper hangings from the thirteenth and fourteenth centuries depict tigers as a protection against evil.

The tiger was the guardian of the dead as well as the living. It frightened away threatening spirits. Its image protected the entrance to tombs. Wood block prints hung up at special times of the year kept bad luck away. Silver amulets bearing the image of the tiger were put on newborn boys in the hope that they would take on responsibility for the family and care for the elders. Before their baby was born, prospective mothers would begin sewing shoes, collars, hats and bibs in many different tiger shapes so as to keep away any spirit that might harm their child. Baby boys are still given tiger hats, collars and shoes at the age of one month, and again after a hundred days, to protect them. Tiger pillows were considered the only remedy for nightmares. The image of a tiger's eye, especially on shoes, would act as a guide, enabling the child to see his way.

In the mountains of Tibet, the people used tiger-skin rugs to ward off snakes, scorpions, insects and other creatures. Those in authority would sit on a tiger rug to pronounce verdicts or mete out punishments. A tiger rug could be part of the ritual adornment of a throne.

When people travelled they would throw a tiger rug over the back of their horse, covering their luggage for protection. Some rugs depicted tigers in pairs, representing the twin concepts of yin and yang. As one writer put it, 'The relevance of the tiger lies in the ambiguous nature of his relationship with man. It mirrors the opposition between men and beasts, nature and civilization, the controlled and the uncontrolled power. He is the spirit that mediates between the world of the living and that of those who have passed on to the beyond. In this concept, the tiger is one who can transcend the boundaries between both realms. It is herein that rests his symbolic power.'

It was not only for its skin that the tiger was hunted. In Chinese medicine, every inch of the tiger's body played a part in the treatment of human illness. A Chinese *Materia Medica* dating from the sixteenth century recommends the use of tiger fat to combat all kinds of vomiting and to treat dog-bite wounds; tiger blood builds up the constitution and strengthens the willpower; its testes can be used to cure scrofula, its bile to calm convulsions in children, even its eyeballs to treat epilepsy and malaria.

The image of the tiger acted as a charm against the influence of spirits. A likeness of the animal in any form was also considered a protection against disease. A tiger's claw averted evil, small bones of the feet were potent charms and prevented convulsions in children, spectral fevers could be cured by touching the skin. Even fevers that had been thought incurable were calmed by reading verses about tigers!

The flesh of the tiger was supposed to prevent stomach and spleen disorders, pills from the eyeballs to cure convulsions. The whiskers and claws provided great strength and courage, and the roasted skin was a cure for all ills, especially when mixed with water. Tiger grease diluted with oil cured stomach ailments, while bones from the end of the tail and floating ribs destroyed evil and brought good fortune.

The Chinese also believed that the tiger had great sexual powers, being able to copulate several times an hour and over a hundred times in the course of a few days. The tiger's penis was therefore considered a most powerful aphrodisiac. Aging Chinese gentlemen though that by eating it they could attain the same prowess.

The question then arises, how did the tiger survive in the wild when its skin and every part of its body were in such demand? It seems likely that China's forests were full of tigers before the advent of the gun. Tigers were certainly trapped and killed throughout the country on special ceremonial occasions, but there was not the large-scale destruction that came with commercial hunting. The lives of men and the image of the tiger were interwoven in the ancient culture of the area. The disintegration of these elements has accelerated over the last hundred years or so as a result of various events in the lives of the forest communities, the forest and the tiger.

In the middle of the nineteenth century, tigers were very common in southern China – indeed, the area has its own subspecies, the South China tiger, which is a little smaller than its Indian counterpart. It roamed the rocky gorges of Changyung and Patung, the valleys of Chienchang and Yunnan and the mountains of Yenpayi. One was even recorded as having swum to the island city of Amoy, where it was eventually killed. A 'black' tiger was reported killed near Hangchow in the Eastern Tombs forest in 1912. Canton, Foochow and Nangking all boasted tiger populations.

But with the arrival of the Europeans, life changed. New weapons, new religions, the booming fur trade, the receding of the forest as land was claimed for agriculture all took their toll on the lives of the forest people and their guardian, the tiger. Another traditional culture was about to fade.

One of the most extraordinary characters in China at this time was a Christian missionary called H. R. Caldwell. He was also a sportsman and a naturalist, and was one of the few people to make a detailed study of the South China tiger. A traveller who met him in Fukien wrote, 'He almost invariably went on foot from place to place and carried with him a butterfly net and a rifle, so that to so keen a naturalist each day's walk was full of interest. During his experiences with the Futsing tigers, Mr Caldwell has learned much about their habits and peculiarities. . . .'

Caldwell's unique achievement in a land where the tiger was common and both black and white tigers had been recorded was to find the only instance ever of a 'blue' tiger. He wrote, 'The markings of the animal were marvellously beautiful. The ground colour seemed to be a deep shade of maltese, changing into almost deep blue on the underparts.'

Caldwell tried unsuccessfully to hunt this tiger; a companion of his, who never actually saw it, wrote, 'I believed then, and my opinion has subsequently been strengthened, that it is a partially melanistic phase of the ordinary yellow tiger.' The local people referred to the tiger as 'bluebeard' or 'black devil' and Caldwell found reference to the 'black devils' many years after his first sighting.

*C*hildren's slippers are still embroidered with 'tiger's eyes' to protect them against any obstacle in their path as they walk. These were made of silk and satin in the early twentieth century. A 'tiger cap' is another charm that will protect children against evil.

The conflict between tiger and dragon generated such ferocity that a thunderstorm would build up and the dry earth would receive vital water.

But Caldwell's principal reason for being in China was to advance the knowledge of Christianity. He spent twenty-four years there, mostly in Fukien, a land full of tigers, where man and tiger had mutual respect. Caldwell's memoir, Blue Tiger, is a remarkable story of how traditional beliefs were wiped out at the beginning of this century. A chapter entitled 'A Rifle as a Calling Card' boasts of the virtues of his fancy gun, a weapon that had never been seen in the area before. He quotes one of his own speeches to the natives he had come to convert: 'Friends, you agree with me that this gun is better than yours and that the American farm implement is better than those with which you cultivate your fields and harvest your grain, and when you have listened to what I have to say about the Christ doctrine, you will see that it too is better than the religions of your fathers.'

In his arrogance, Caldwell thought he could change belief with his gun. In an area where tigers were revered because the people believed their supernatural energies had to be propitiated, he slaughtered them at every opportunity. He records with pride that an elder from one of the forest communities once said to him, 'Teacher, I am afraid those people would not have heard of Christ until this day had you not killed that tiger.'

What did this do to the way of life of the people? Did a conflict of new religions spread by the Europeans tear into traditional beliefs? Did the tiger and the forest suffer with the arrival of guns? Must Christianity take some responsibility for the scarring of nature that occurred as man reaffirmed his role as 'supreme being'? One thing is certain: Over the last two centuries, a way of life in Asia, in the land of the tiger, was rocked to its foundations, especially by men like Caldwell.

As the twentieth century progressed and communism held sway over China, the importance of cultivation was stressed so that the land would produce more. Like so many political systems, this ignored the fine balance that existed between man and nature and the links between the past and the present. By the middle of this century, many wild creatures in China, including the tiger, had been declared pests. Hunters were encouraged to kill tigers and paid a bounty for each one. It was only in 1977 that the government woke up to the fact that the tiger population had decreased alarmingly and banned tiger hunting altogether. Such a law is, of course, almost impossible to enforce, and a black market in tigers is now the overriding cause for the decline in its population. There are something between fifty and seventy-five South China tigers left, and the tiger will probably soon be extinct throughout China.

INTO INDO-CHINA

The tiger's remarkable swimming prowess made it an occasional visitor to Hong Kong, crossing from mainland China at points where the distance between the two is only one kilometre. An account by a former prisoner of war published in the *South China Morning Post* in 1951 documented some of the sightings:

'Nearly every winter one or more tigers visit the New Territories; often the visitor is a tigress with or without cubs. The visit rarely lasts more than two or three days. A tiger thinks nothing of a forty mile walk and in a couple of nights could walk from the wild country behind Bias Bay to Tai Mo Shao or the Kowloon hills. Because their visits are usually of such short duration and because most people exaggerate, little credence is given to tiger rumours. . . .

'During our internment at Stanley, a remarkable story filtered into our camp that there was a tiger at large on Hong Kong island. Later it was reported to be on Stanley peninsula; our Formosan guards got very excited and it was risky walking about in the evening, for an excited guard might fire at a prisoner, mistaking him for a tiger. Soon pugmarks were seen in the camp. I examined them myself, but was by no means convinced. Then the story was spread that the tiger had been shot and finally there came into camp a Chinese or Japanese paper containing a photograph of the dead tiger. This photograph I saw. People said that it was a menagerie animal that had got loose – a likely story! It is strange how loth people are to believe that tigers do visit the colony and occasionally swim the harbour and visit the island.'

The skin of this tiger is still to be found in the Tun Han temple in Stanley village.

But Hong Kong was never really part of the tiger's territory. From southern China it advanced through Indo-China, entering Vietnam, Laos and Cambodia and probably at the same time extending its range through Burma and India.

Stepping into Vietnam, the tiger entered another world. The country stretches over 1,600 kilometres from the misty mountains on the Chinese border to the flat Mekong delta in the south: in between lie various bays where strangely shaped lime rock mountains jut out of the emerald sea while fishing junks ply in and out of the quiet waters. The highland regions offer majestic views of jungle-covered mountains and primeval tropical forests. On the delta the sun is fierce, and cool shade is provided by banana and coconut trees. One early writer evoked it thus:

'In the high plateau of the Moi hinterland lying in the centre of Indo-China where Vietnam, Cambodia and Laos all meet, the forest clearings are always covered with pines and other conifers. In South Vietnam, in the neighbourhood of Phanrang, the general desolation of the scenery is enhanced by the fantastic bare silhouettes of stunted trees standing up gaunt in the grassy plain. This kind of country crops up again at Son Phan, an area near the border of South Annam which is very rich in game of all kinds, especially the big grey ox and the little red one. In Cambodia, these clearings are often visited by cow-prey and in Laos by a smaller species of gaur. Deer, goats, muntjacs, wild boar and agoutis are usually to be found in the forest clearing; so also is the tiger, who comes here to escape from the wood-leech, elsewhere so abundant.'

It was in this land that the tiger encountered the forest-dwelling people known as the Mnong or Moi. Like so many other peoples throughout Asia, their lives were deeply rooted in the forest, giving and taking under the umbrella of nature – until the arrival of the Europeans. An incident which occurred towards the end of the nineteenth century is typical of the conflict that Western influence brought.

A scientific survey required the cutting down of a tree. The chief of the Mnong 'coolies' employed to help the scientists approached the tree and addressed it with these words: 'Spirit who last made thy home in this tree, we worship thee and come to claim thy mercy. The white mandarin, our relentless master, whose commands we cannot but obey, has bidden us to cut down thy habitation, a task that fills us with sadness and which we only carry out with regret. I adjure thee to depart at once from the place and seek a new dwelling place elsewhere, and I pray thee to forget the wrong we do thee, for we are not our own masters.'

This speech was accompanied by a complete obeisance and concluded by another to the king of the forest, the tiger, who has jurisdiction over each tree in the area. The Mnong believe that the tiger is first among animals and has great supernatural powers. They refer to him with respect and fear, calling him king of the mountain, his eminence, my lord, the gentleman, the master or lofty one, rather than use the word tiger.

Once while trapping deer the Mnong caught a tiger in their trap. Terrified that it might die, they lowered a cage and ropes into the pit and lifted the tiger out, with profuse apologies for having kept it so long in such conditions.

On another occasion, a tiger who had killed a man was forgiven by the man's family with the words, 'My brother should know that the spirits of my relations who never received burial nor the rites that were their due have long demanded another companion.' It was genuinely believed that the tiger would only kill a man who had committed a sin.

Sometimes a ceremony was conducted at the spot where a tiger had killed a man. The image of a tiger with three figures on its back was drawn on a piece of paper; the paper was then solemnly burned and the fine ashes scattered over the tomb amid much prayer and reverence. Memorial stones for the tiger were also erected in such places, with the image of the tiger painted on the stone. The altar in the tomb had a niche where joss sticks were burned to please the spirit of the tiger and the forest – any passerby would stop to pray and make some sort of offering.

The Mnong believed that the power of the tiger's whiskers could create a fatal poison. The whiskers were enclosed in hollow bamboo sticks. After many watches, a snake would emerge; once a year the medicine man would feed the snake grains of maize, and the snake would provide drops of poison. The poison had to be used by a certain time against whoever the spirits chose. Other parts of the tiger's body were regarded as beneficial in much the same way as they are in Chinese medicine. In particular, the small bones in the shoulder were worn as a charm to protect the wearer from danger in the forest.

A tiger which was clumsy enough to damage the ear of its victim in an attack would abandon it immediately and never return to eat it, said the Mnong, and when a tiger killed a man it lost a bit of its own ear. The chunks missing from a tiger's ear indicated the number of its victims. Another facet of Mnong belief asserted that the tiger could hear anything said about him 'even from a thousand leagues away' and was quick to avenge any insult. The tiger's ability to transform itself into a human being and speak was an integral part of their thinking. They were always delighted when they saw a tiger yawn, especially at noon: it meant that he was relieving his memory and spitting out anything that had been said against him. It was like frequently wiping the slate clean, and the Mnong were grateful for this.

The spirit of the grain was invoked before every harvest in a complicated ritual in which the sacrifice of a pig or chicken completed the offering to the spirit. This worship of the grain was interwoven with the worship of the tiger so as to provide a rich harvest from a fertile soil.

If evil spirits had caused physical or mental illness, a shaman was called on to expel the spirit. An early traveller described what happened:

'To the accompaniment of a series of peculiar writhing movements, she chants a litany which gets quicker and quicker as the candles get smaller. Her contortions also become more rapid and violent and in the end she is seized with a fit of hysterics, which signifies the frantic struggle of the "Pi" before they yield to the power of the incantation. All at once her movement ceases and she commences to indicate the hour in which the cure will take place.'

The importance of the tiger in the life of the Mnong was evident from the many ways in which they used a dead tiger or one that had been captured for ritual occasions. Teeth and claws provided charms to ward off evil. Teeth were also filed to produce a powder that cured dog bites. When a man-eater was killed (usually by European hunters), a cigarette holder was made from one of its canines so that it would reveal the victim's image when it was blackened by the smoke. The nerves were carefully cleaned and mixed with alcohol to produce an elixir for long life and a potent aphrodisiac – another link between the tiger, fertility and immortality.

One Englishman who hunted many tigers with the Mnong remarked on their uncanny reverence for the animal: 'Despite the depredations of these thieving old tigers, these villagers never take any sensible steps to get rid of them. The local magicians may see these man-eaters as unfortunate creatures haunted by departed spirits thirsting for vengeance, and if that is their view, these tigers must not be hunted: they must instead be treated with every respect and consideration. The magician has been known to carry this farce to the point where the villagers have been exhorted to leave their homes altogether so as to avoid upsetting the spirits. The result has been a mass migration.'

After a tiger had attacked a Mnong woman, the same observer wrote, 'The man-eater had a strange preference for the opposite sex, since in five weeks he had taken two women before this one. The magician spoke of "metempsychosis" (the passing of the soul after death into another body). According to him, this tiger was inhabited by the soul of a deceased husband. That was enough for the Moi. A wave of marital fidelity immediately swept through the village and all the married folk enjoyed, thanks to the tiger, a second honeymoon!

'But somewhere the Moi believed that the presence of tiger was virtuous in spirit or reality. They knew that when their crops were being destroyed by other animals, it was always the tiger that stepped in to provide justice. The tiger often helped them to preserve a piece of rice or maize in some isolated square of mountainous region. They revered it as a gentleman.'

Strict taboos governed childbirth and the wrath of the tiger might be visited on anyone who failed to observe them. Incest was punished by wishing for attack by the tiger of violent death. Lightning was believed to strike the guilty party in the form of the dragon that flayed, the tiger that devoured and the elephant that impaled.

Legends concerning the tiger featured in every facet of Mnong life. There was a story about a tiger who was on the verge of devouring a cow. The cow begged to be spared as she had a calf to suckle. The calf then implored the tiger to eat her soft flesh rather than her mother's tough old hide. Each insisted on being the victim until the tiger, overwhelmed by this tenderness, sent both away without harming them.

The forests that the Mnong inhabited have been decimated, but one woman who had followed the tiger from India to Burma to Java and Sumatra and finally to Vietnam, where she succeeded in shooting one, described the habitat as she saw it:

'The trees were about sixty years old and some distance to the north another forest began, rather sharply differentiated, with trees a hundred years old, and further north were other forests yet older, as if the armies of great pines, marching south from China, were flinging out battalions of young trees ahead of them.

'They were very wonderful, those walks through the jungle at night. I think we were quite mad in what we did, though we liked to think then that we were being cautious, moving carefully and keeping a wary outlook. The lights on our heads made the rest of the world utterly dark, though the soft stars were pouring down a still radiance. We moved through a black velvet scene, the headlights picking one object at a time out of the gloom, now the round bole of a pine tree, now a feathery shrub, now a plumed spear of waving grass.... Very often we heard the startled snort of some astonished beast. Once a stag crashed out of the depths of a dewy thicket where it had been asleep. We stopped softly, the night wind blowing in our faces, attended only by that ghostly ray of light in the vast darkness.... We had an extraordinary sense of solitude.

'Out of the wall of distant shadows came a gleam of gold and black – vivid as lighting against the green – and the tiger walked out of the jungle. Never in my life had I seen such a picture. Elephants by moonlight, lions at dawn, gorillas at blazing noon I had seen, but nothing was ever so beautiful and so glorious to me as that tiger walking out of his jungle. He was everything that was wild and savage, lordly and sinister. 'He seemed to materialize like something in a dream and for a moment I could imagine I was dreaming. He stood, projected vividly against the forest, and he looked enormous. The great striped roundness of him was like a barrel. Then he moved, and seemed to flow along the ground, nearer and nearer.'

A Frenchman travelling in the same area observed a fascinating instance of communal living among one group of tigers:

'Before us lay a great jumble of rocks, surmounted by an immense bare plateau. An astonishing labyrinth, born of one of nature's wildest dreams, was split into innumerable cracks and heaped into fantastic blocks of incredible shapes and sizes. Here and there the rocks were banded together with clay, but for the most part it was a colossal jumble of loose boulders and great yawning chasms. In several places the rock face was hollowed into shallow caves, reached by steep, rocky little tracks which could possibly be used by a tiger; one of them, bigger than the rest, looked as though it might be the main entrance to the caves. The earth all round was clear of all grass and had no doubt been worn smooth by the tigers' feet.

'Actually there was only one complete family living here – the tigress, her cubs and the big tiger my friend shot. Another tiger – the one I accounted for – lived by himself in a separate apartment, and the last tigress lived in another cul-de-sac with the baby whose body we found. The maze of caverns and passages provided a safe retreat, sheltered from bad weather, and they would sally forth separately at night to scour the countryside, keeping as far as possible out of one another's way.'

The same writer reflected nostalgically on his time in Indo-China: 'So remote seemed all the deceptive activity, all the squalid restlessness of civilization that life there with my Moi friends seemed to be out of this world. They were primitive and simple-minded, and in their company I spent the happiest hours of my life, reading in the great open book of nature, seeking always to probe its mysteries and discover its secrets. Now I am buried deep – against my will – in the noisy whirl of a great city and I find myself longing once more for that clean and healthy freedom of body and soul which I knew in the luxuriant forests or on the limitless savannahs where the giant crickets used to sing their discordant songs.'

Again, hunters found the local people reluctant to help them hunt tigers: the attempt alone was regarded as a sign of disrespect for which the whole village would suffer later on. Losing a member of the village on such an expedition would be disastrous, for if the bones were not found and a suitable burial ceremony not conducted, the spirit in its agony would seek revenge for generations to come. Hunters would find small altars and temples deep in the forest, where images of the tiger would remind them of the reverence with which the Mnong treated this awesome creature.

Violence has ravaged Indo-China for decades. Napalm has destroyed huge tracts of forest and hundreds of thousands of lives have been lost. With the return of some semblance of peace in recent years, tigers have been discovered surviving in pockets of forest throughout the area. It is said that they survived the devastations of war and that their numbers might have increased since they fed on the many people who lay dead deep within the forests. There may be 200 or 300 tigers left. If, as some claim, the forest-dwellers of Vietnam have killed some of the few remaining, they are surely not to be blamed. The last hundred years of dealing with death, destruction and the devastation of their traditional wisdom and way of life must have created unimaginable turmoil. And the responsibility for this lies elsewhere.

INTO THAILAND

The tiger next squeezed into Thailand. The 1,500 kilometres of land from north to south encompass diverse climates – the north a part of the monsoon belt with long dry periods and the south tropical in flavour with frequent rainfall and endless coasts, beaches and bays. On the borders of Thailand, Laos and Cambodia, the forest peoples believed that if they ate certain types of wild rice they could change into tigers and that if women rubbed magical ointment on their bodies and rushed into the forest they could change into tigresses in seven days. The Khon Lamoh people of Thailand also thought men could turn into tigers by using magical formulas. These beliefs seemed to become more prevalent as the tiger moved further south.

One of the last refuges of the tiger in Thailand is the Khao Yai National Park, mountainous country with peaks as high as 1,350 metres. The area receives two monsoons a year and the average rainfall is an extraordinary 3,000 mm. Most of the park is covered by dry or semi-evergreen rain forests, while the mountainsides are cloaked with evergreens. Despite this ideal tiger habitat, populations are decreasing. In 1977 there were an estimated 500–600 tigers in Thailand; now there may be 250 or even fewer.

INTO MALAYSIA

An early traveller in the Malay forests described a tiger hunt and the weapons used by the Malays to beat a forest: 'Such men as owned, or had been able to borrow, a small dagger of a peculiar shape known as a *golok rembau* exhibited their weapons with complacency and pride; for these daggers are supposed by the Malay to possess such extraordinary, even magical properties that a tiger is powerless against them.

'When the local chief announced that everything was ready, an old *pawang* stepped forward with a punch of twigs of a tree for which a tiger is thought to have a peculiar dread. Holding this small bundle in both hands, he repeated over it the charm known as "that which closes the tiger's mouth", and then, after another incantation which was intended to prevent the tiger from winding us, proceeded to break the twigs into short fragments, which he distributed first among the shooters and then among the beaters. The ceremony did not take long, but by the time it was over and the final words of advice, exhortation and command had been said on every side, the sun was strong enough to make the shade welcome; and without further delay the old chief led his picturesque throng of beaters down one path, while we set off along a track that took us into another part of the forest.'

As they progressed through the forest, there was a sudden pause: 'There was silence for a moment, and then a great voice shouted, "*Selawat*" (prayer). "*Selawat!*" shouted everyone; and thereupon one of the men in the long line chanted aloud some verses of the Koran, concluding by shouting at the top of his voice the words of the creed of Islam, "There is no God but Allah and Muhammad is the prophet of Allah." And from every voice in the array that was hidden up and down the forest came the roar of the response of the final Allah. Apart from its religious aspect, the use of the *selawat* is to enable the men to know whereabouts in the denseness and tangle of the forest undergrowth the animal is hidden.

'Before long the cry arose again: "Here he is! Here he is!" Upon this the old chief in charge of the drive shouted an order: "Steady. Hold steady." Down on a knee dropped every man of the 200 that composed the line. Close to his side, each man gripped his spear, with its point thrust upwards into the dark forest undergrowth in front of him.

'The excitement by this time was almost overpowering in its intensity. I could not, of course, see the men, but knew by the sound that only this distance separated us and that on the other side of the thickets and tree-trunks in front of me fierce Malay eyes glared and peered for the hidden tiger. Then suddenly, in a tree halfway between the beaters and the guns, a squirrel raised its chattering note of alarm. Another squirrel immediately took up the cry, and the pair of them kept up such an incessant excited clamour that it was plain that they were scolding an intruder; it was obvious, too, that the intruder was within a few yards of them.

'The nearer of the beaters heard it and dropped on their knees, with their spears thrust forward to receive it. "Here he is! Here he is! Steady! Hold steady!"

'For a space not a man moved: probably not a man breathed. Then I shouted that the animal that had come out was only a pig, and that the tiger had not yet shown itself. "Pig!" they roared up and down the line. "Only a pig."

'But whatever the average person's feelings may be regarding the race of cats, there is little doubt that almost everyone has a peculiar sensation of the almost god-like beauty, power, activity and strength of a tiger.'

This 'god-like beauty' created a faith in magic, in were-tigers and in the spirits that haunted the forest. Another hunter experienced some of the strength of these beliefs. In order to shoot a man-eater, he had to consult the *pawang* or medicine man of the village. The *pawang* in turn organized a ceremony to confer with the spirits. A goat was sacrificed and the blood saved from coagulation. The meat was divided into three portions and cooked with rice, one for the *pawang*, one for the forest spirit and one for the tiger spirit. In the night, the *pawang* was surrounded by various charms, shells and even the clothing of the tiger's victims. He offered a prayer to the lord of the heavens and the spirit of the forest, seeking their permission to search for the man-eater. He ended the ceremony with a prayer to Allah.

His chanting grew louder as he dropped various charms into the blood. The blood bubbled and there ensued a terrific struggle between the *pawang* and the spirit, accompanied by shrieks, snarls and other animal sounds. Amidst loud cries, the *pawang* thrust the spirit into the glowing charcoal and collapsed in a heap. When he opened his eyes he informed the hunter that the forest spirit had given permission for the tiger to be killed, but only after an animal with one eye missing had been shot. There was also the proviso that if the hot rains fell, the hunt would have to be stopped – otherwise, a chief's son would be sacrificed.

The hunter went off the next day and encountered a wild boar, which he shot. On examining the corpse he found that it had one eye missing. Shortly afterwards it started raining and the hunt discovered and shot a snarling tiger. Later the hunter found that it had killed and half devoured a chief's son. 'Was it coincidence again, or fate?' he wrote. 'I don't venture to explain the episode, but I know from actual records the Malay *pawangs* have made even more uncanny predictions which have been inexplicably fulfilled.'

The tiger was lord of the Malay jungles, always referred to as 'the striped prince' or 'old hairy face', never by the name tiger, which he would have regarded as an insult. When a Malay came across tiger tracks in the jungle, he covered them with leaves and twigs to prove that he had shown due deference. As lord of the jungle, the tiger was very much a part of the ritual and well-being of the people. Seances among the Benua people show how inextricably linked people, forests and tigers are.

The object of the seance is to cure – a shaman, the intermediary between the people and the heaven above, is about to evoke the spirit of the tiger. He sits quietly, completely covered up in the magical circle. His eyes peer out. The drumbeat gets louder and louder, taking over from the sharp sounds of the crickets. A candle flame starts to quiver. The tiger spirit has arrived – this is how it is manifested. It has entered the candle and the shaman's eyes are fixed on the flame, unblinking, unwavering. The tiger spirit has descended on him to provide the cure. The shaman soon shakes with a frenzy, driving away evil and all the demons around. He growls, snarls and leaps much like a tiger, then falls into a state of *lupa* or unconsciousness. He is now in communication with the spirit. The cure has started. This is Malay shamanism, in which the tiger spirit is invoked as the mythical ancestor and initiatory master of the entire area.

As the well-known anthropologist Mircea Eliade put it, 'The *pawang* did in effect turn himself into a tiger; he ran on all fours, roared and licked the patient's body for a long time as a tigress licks her cubs.'

A small cluster of huts surrounded by thick, unending Malayan jungle makes up a tiny Negrito pygmy village. The Negritos are hunter-gatherers, living very much as they have always done, in balance with nature, taking little and giving much.

It is dusk and the sky is slowly darkening. Someone is seriously ill. The *halak* or medicine man has retired to his tiny leaf hut to invoke the *cenoi* – the nephews of God. Time passes. Suddenly from the hut the voices of the *cenoi* rise in a crescendo. The *halak* has started singing and speaking in an unknown language. The hut seems to be shaking. The spirits have descended to reveal the cause of the illness. The seance has begun.

The *halak* passes out threads made of palm leaves so as to reach Bonsu, the celestial god who dwells above the seven levels of the sky. The *halak* is now connected by these threads to the god above. The *cenoi* give him quartz crystals which symbolize the celestial vault and the sky gods. The *halak* peers into these crystals to seek a cure. In the crystals he suddenly sees a tiger approaching. This is the first phase of the cure.

The *halak* is a man who has the ability to enter a trance or be possessed by a spirit. The Negritos believe that when a *halak* dies he becomes a tiger, but a tiger that will never harm his own people. Only when he has lived out the lifespan of a tiger will his soul enter the next world.

The Malays fear the Negritos, whom they think are all were-tigers. The Negritos believe in two souls – the life spirit and the dream soul. During life, the dream soul leaves the body at night and can wander round as a tiger, capturing the excitement of the dream. The life spirit dies when the body dies, but soon after the burial rituals are over the dream soul journeys into another world.

The transformation of man to tiger occurs through the medium of water. Tigers swim through lakes and rivers to turn themselves into people and even when they are turning back into tigers, water is essential. Sometimes magical yellow sarongs with black stripes are used to effect such a transition. The Negritos regard the tiger as the son of the thunder god Karei, thus connecting the tiger to water, rain and regeneration – a parallel to the Chinese belief that the tiger and the dragon worked in conjunction to create rain.

If someone is killed by a tiger, the Negritos accept this philosophically: the tiger is seen as the executor of special punishments for those who sin.

Similar stories abound among the various native peoples of Malaysia – seances evoking tiger spirits were an integral part of their traditional culture. In fact, the Malays were far more in awe of tiger spirits than of the living creatures.

In these areas, the invocation of the tiger spirit seemed to create a sense of well-being and harmony. It activated a kind of 'togetherness' in the individual – perhaps because the ecstatic journeys that were vividly portrayed by the shaman, where super-natural forces gradually became visible and revealed a recognizable form, conveyed some knowledge about death or a moment beyond reality. Instead of being something terrifying and unfamiliar, death could be seen as a gradual passage to a spiritual state of being, in which the tiger spirit played a major role.

Stories of were-tigers are widespread, probably based on ancient Malay legends about tigers turning themselves into men. One tale concerns a visitor to a village who fell ill and vomited a large number of feathers. His host was not surprised, as the previous day a tiger had entered the village and killed many chickens – the ailing visitor was obviously a 'tiger man'. On other occasions, men were found in traps set for tigers, but the only marks on the ground around the trap were those of a tiger.

Many Malays believe that there are tiger villages deep in the jungle where tiger men live in houses and behave like human beings. Their house-posts are made of tree nettles, the roofs are thatched with human hair, men's bones are the only rafters and their skins make the walls. These tiger men seem to live peacefully most of the time, in between periodic attacks on carefully selected prey. A number of these villages are supposed to exist near the Straits of Malacca.

Among the population of Jempul, certain families are considered 'tiger families'. Members of these families turn into tigers after death. They are supposed to be related to real tigers living in the forest who in times of crisis will appear to protect cattle or poultry from attack and even to guard the paddy fields against the ravages of wild boar. If a member of one of these families falls ill, a tiger is always seen around the house. It is completely harmless, having come simply to express its concern at its relative's ill health.

There is a legend about a *balak* who went to shoot with his blow-pipe. While he was away, his wife roasted fruit to feed to her hungry child. Burning fruit was taboo, and it exploded. Custom demanded that a tiger eat the offender, so the woman's father-in-law turned into a tiger and did so. Such legends create a sense of ritual within the communities which is understandably strictly observed.

Another legend concerns an extremely large tiger which has lived in the jungle for many centuries. No one ever sees it, but occasionally huge tracks are found. When its great roar is heard in the dry season, it is a sure prognostication of rain in fifteen days' time.

Malays also believe that tigers never attack human beings from the front: on every person's forehead is inscribed a verse from the Koran proclaiming man's superiority over the animals, and the tiger is unable to face this inscription!

It was off the coast of Malaysia that fishermen eight kilometres out to sea once came across a dark object moving on the surface of the water. It turned out to be a fully grown tiger, which they netted and drowned. This is the only record of a tiger being sighted so far from land, and is an extraordinary testimony to its swimming ability.

The tiger population in Malaysia is today estimated at 650. In the 1950s it was nearly 3,000. Because of the massive clearing of forests over the last decades, its stronghold is now the Taman Negara tropical forest, which it shares with a few hundred Negritos. Their expertise in analysing the forest language comes from a vast reservoir of traditional knowledge accumulated over many generations; they are today a vital source of assistance to anyone conducting a scientific study there. If this remarkable area were left to the Negritos, the tiger would surely continue to prosper – but with increasing human pressures, this seems hardly likely to happen.

INTO SUMATRA

The tiger's expertise in water took it to Singapore centuries ago, and it seems to have flourished. A guide book to the area written in the early nineteenth century states that tigers were so numerous that passengers arriving on steamers could see them at the water's edge. One writer produced an interesting theory about why it should have been attracted there: 'It is difficult to conceive what can induce tigers to cross over to Singapore; for although there are a few deer and plenty of pigs on the island, there is a much greater variety of game in the Johore peninsula. Can it be a taste for human flesh, which is more plentiful in the island?'

It is fascinating to speculate whether tigers regularly swam back and forth across the straits and whether Singapore can be considered part of their individual territories.

On at least one large island in South-East Asia, Borneo, there is no scientific evidence of the presence of tigers, though local legends make it seem likely that tigers did once live there. But Indonesia was a recognized part of the tiger's territory.

The tiger moved there long, long ago, perhaps walking across while the islands were still attached to mainland Asia, perhaps swimming to Sumatra in the days when the distance involved was only fifteen to twenty kilometres. If a tiger has been recorded eight kilometres out to sea off Malaysia, this is surely not impossible.

Whatever the origins of the Sumatran tiger, its home is steeped in tiger lore – were-tigers, tiger villages and deep-rooted rituals linking tiger and man. Indonesia is a land of volcanoes, of rain forests and thick, dark, inaccessible mangrove swamps. The eruption of Krakatoa in 1883 killed nearly 40,000 people, and the crew of a ship found tiger corpses floating 200 kilometres out to sea.

When the Dutch colonists arrived, tigers were flourishing throughout Sumatra, as one nineteenth-century traveller found to his surprise: 'My horse sud-

A tiger motif on the cloth known as patola. It is known to have been made in Gujarat in India in the eighteenth century, but was found in Indonesia. The fascination with tigers spread, regardless of language, religion or culture, throughout the tiger's range.

denly snorted in a strange manner and came to a dead stop with its feet planted in the ground, then reared back; at the same moment the great body of a tiger shot close past my face and alighted with a heavy thud in the jungle on my other side. Haunted with the idea that I was perhaps being stalked, the night became doubly dismal to me.'

Belief in human beings who were able to change themselves into tigers was widespread. These people seemed totally normal except that they lacked the groove in the upper lip; in their tiger form they were completely harmless. One European found that a family of tigers had invaded his property by night:

'On the right, in the dark by the bamboos, gleamed the eyes of a big tiger; nearer the entrance two cubs were playing round the recumbent tigress. It would have been a pretty picture in a zoo, seen beyond good strong bars, but I could only feel a thrill of horror. And the next night, *"Thuan, thuan."* I jumped out of bed, picked up my gun, turned up the lamp and hurried into the dining room.

'The tigers were there again. The biggest one was lying on the edge of the enclosure and the cubs were jumping about. The tigress stood with her head erect and her tail stretched out, and her eyes fixed on the servants. My heart beat violently as I raised my gun. I was about to shoot, but something seemed to hold me back. The tigers were doing nobody any harm.

'On moonlit nights I saw them playing in the enclosure, innocently and good-humouredly like great cats. Gradually I got used to them. The tigers never did the slightest harm: on the contrary, they did me a great service, for now when I was unable to get back at night, no thief ever ventured anywhere near my house.'

The forest people were obviously impressed by the European who had been thus singled out by tigers:

'At kampong festivals, presents of food were sent to me. The people kept me supplied with all sorts of good things – fruit, eggs and river fishes. They greeted me almost reverently as I passed them. In short, I was treated like a prince, though I was a very ragged one, with my patched khaki clothes and clay-soiled hobnailed boots.'

The tiger family arrived to play and rest nearly every night over a period of months. Then a guest at the home tried – unsuccessfully – to shoot one of them. The tigers disappeared and never came back. Were these tigers, or humans in tiger form?

Natives of peninsular Malaysia and Sumatra believed that somewhere deep in the forests of Sumatra, the Korinchi people lived in tiger villages and could turn themselves into tigers at dusk, then back to human beings at dawn. As elsewhere, these transformations took place in water, which was regarded as the essence of life, so bathing in it was a good omen. The tiger was regarded as the son of the thunder god – another association with rain and fertility.

Elsewhere in Sumatra certain people were believed to have the ability to turn into tigers, especially if a member of their family had for some reason been killed by a tiger. The intense feeling of loss would suddenly cause the surviving relative to develop fur and claws; he would then rush into the forest. He was only able to become human again if he was rolled in a special cloth.

The Batak people believed that the souls of their ancestors resided in the tiger, so they would never kill it or eat its flesh. Members of the clan were supposed to be descended from tigers and after death their souls would turn back into tigers. Tigers were believed to live near tombs, but were only visible to those who had not sinned. Royalty, nobility and courageous warriors claimed descent from the white tiger, and the grave of a former sultan is supposed to be guarded by a white tiger which appears every Thursday to receive offerings and grant requests. Killing a tiger was believed to cause death and havoc from floods, volcanic eruptions, other natural disasters and even accidents.

In an area of strong Islamic influence, Allah gave the tiger as protection only to his special followers; the graves of holy Muslims were guarded by tigers. Anyone who transgressed the commands of Islam would be punished by the intervention of the tiger. The tiger was so deeply rooted in local beliefs that Islam must have had to embrace it much as Buddhism did in Korea. As late as 1951, when a hundred people died as a result of tiger attacks, it was seen as the vengeance of Allah. The tiger only devoured those who had committed evil deeds.

The Sumatran legend about the origin of the tiger is fascinating. A newly wed couple were making love in their hut in the middle of a rice field. The man was about to climax when they heard someone approaching. He withdrew while ejaculating and some of his sperm fell on the earth. It turned into a tiger and disappeared into the forest, where it remained.

It was commonly believed in Sumatra that the tiger did not bother man unless man bothered him. The few tigers that raided villages were thought to have been banished by their own societies and to be unable to return to normal life as tigers within the forest. The Sumatrans said that such decisions were taken where there was a gathering of tigers and that there was a king of the tigers who wore a chain of palm leaves as a sign of his office.

In one part of the island sacrifices of water buffalo were offered to the tiger so that he would protect the pepper plantations and rice fields. After this ritual feast, the tiger would protect the crops against other animals and the villagers would have few worries until harvest time. There was a weekly tiger holiday during which the tiger entered the village of which he was guardian. Anyone who worked on that day was likely to meet with an accident. Benevolent tigers and tiger spirits would also guard the water buffalo against the raids of 'banished' tigers.

The Gayo people of Sumatra called the tiger the grandfather of the forests; the Kubu regarded it as their best friend. In Minangkabau if a tiger had to be trapped for any reason, the process would be accompanied by prayers in Arabic, bamboo-flute music and a variety of tiger-capturing songs that might entice the tiger into his cage. If the creature in question was a female, she might be lured by a song suggesting that her lover was already in the cage awaiting her.

Shamans were considered to be close relatives of the tiger or to have the ability to turn into one. The shaman was depicted herding flocks of tigers rather than buffaloes. He linked the village in the forest to the tiger by invoking tiger spirits, which also connected the living with the world of the dead, greatly reducing the finality of death and creating a feeling of immortality in that the spirit was deemed to be moving from one world to another.

Links with the tiger even travelled into the art of self-defence known as *silat minang-kabau*, traditionally practised over much of Sumatra. It is based on the tiger's movements and the 'master' who taught this art was said to be related to the tiger.

When the Dutch East India Company arrived in Sumatra the tiger was so numerous that the colonists offered a generous reward for each animal killed. Thousands of tigers have been slaughtered since. In 1978 there were nearly a thousand tigers on the island, in habitat including tropical rain forest, riverine forest, swamp forest and grassland. Today, the number is probably between 300 and 700, a frighteningly low figure for the second most viable tiger population in the world. With the future of the forest in doubt because of large-scale logging operations, there must also be a question mark over the tiger's chances of survival.

INTO JAVA

Across a few kilometres of sea from Sumatra is the home of the Javan tiger, one of the smallest subspecies in the world. It is on this island that tiger fossils dating from the Pleistocene period have been discovered. A European travelling in Java in the late nineteenth century wrote, 'Especially in the centre of the island there are tigers whose ravages are still considerable. Lightning and tigers are the two greatest terrors of the Javanese: he speaks of them only with fearful respect; their victims amount to hundreds each year, yet the natives abstain from any systematic campaign against the tigers, despite the terrors which they inspire, because the destruction of the tigers results, in their experiences, in the advent of herds of wild pigs which ruin the crops.'

There are few recorded instances of Europeans sighting a Javan tiger, but they are full of excitement: 'Minute after minute passed without anything happening. Those minutes seemed to us eternities – eternities of the utmost nervous tension. Our eyes burned as we strained them in searching the edge of the reeds.

'Suddenly we heard behind us the snapping of a dry twig. Without us noticing anything, the tiger had passed along the reed-field and was now behind us. This was unexpected and an unpleasant situation. It was now essential that at least one of us should turn round, but that was almost impossible without making a noise. It had to be done, therefore, as slowly and cautiously as possible. I turned my head round millimetre by millimetre, but I could not turn it far enough to see in the right direction. Meanwhile I had the unpleasant feeling down my back that the tiger was watching us from behind, at the moment perhaps only in curiosity, but perhaps also calculating whether it could leap up to our platform. . . .

'Suddenly I realized that I was looking at the tiger's eyes. Uncertainly and deceptively there gleamed two greenish, spectral eyes in the darkness. They disappeared and then came back into view, remained a while and disappeared again.'

Man, tiger and forest were united in a close friendship affording each party mutual protection. Man was dissuaded from 'stealing' wood or other forest produce by fear of the tiger, and the forest concealed the tiger from the hunter.

Although the Javan tiger may well be extinct, it lives on in myths and legends, rituals and beliefs. The forest communities believed that the souls of their ancestors resided in tigers and refused to harm them or help the Europeans hunt them. Today they still refuse to assist in the poaching of rhinoceros and may yet preserve it from extinction.

In Gumpul in western Java, the spirit of a prince was supposed to have taken the form of a white tiger and guarded the people of the surrounding area. The Sundanese regarded were-tigers of nobles and princes as protective spirits who continued to rule and kept a link between past and present. Since the souls of ancestors resided in the tiger, even the raising of animals with striped or spotted fur was prohibited. Blood was considered a powerful locator of the soul and if a man-eater was killed by a hunter the family who had lost someone to the tiger would attempt to bathe in the tiger's blood so that the tiger's soul could become part of the person.

Sumatra and Java are perhaps more rich in 'tiger connections', with legends of tiger spirits, tiger villages and tiger families, than any other part of the tiger's range. It is almost as if here, at the furthestmost edge of the land of the tiger, it was trying to compensate for the remoteness of the area by having an even more intense involvement with man.

The tiger is almost certainly extinct in Java, but it lives on in the traditional shadow theatre. The cut-out trees on either side represent the tree of life of which the tiger was guardian.

INTO BALI

The smallest subspecies of tiger was found in Bali, where it probably became extinct in 1937, but again the folklore survives. Here, the tiger is closely associated with the Hindu god Brahma, and the goddess Pulaki is depicted followed by three tigers who have the power to possess men. The Balinese mythological beast, the *barong*, sometimes takes the form of a tiger and is depicted draped in scarlet material with stylized stripes.

The Leyak people of Bali were said to feed on corpses which could change their physical form and transform them into tigers. These were-tigers were distinguished, when in human form, by the absence of the groove in the upper lip – a detail common to were-tiger legends throughout South-East Asia. In one battle, Balinese soldiers were said to have spread fear through the enemy ranks by changing into tigers.

At least one European writer had the sensitivity to respond to the links between tiger and man in this last tract of the tiger's domain: 'I have told you some of the strange things in the wilderness that continually fill the life there with new surprises,' he wrote. 'It makes a difference to a man's life there how he treats these things, whether he takes them at all seriously or dismisses them at once with a sceptical smile. The people of the wilderness are alienated by the latter attitude and become taciturn when faced with it; but if one is ready to listen to them without any show of prejudice one will hear many things about the life in the virgin forests that reveal a realm full of beauty and happiness.'

Unfortunately, all too few people shared this tolerance for a different form of wisdom and a different way of being. But Indonesia was a land of the sea-going tiger: it moved freely from one island to another. Even though three distinct subspecies have been recognized in Indonesia, the whole business of the subspecies needs to be further researched, and even questioned.

INTO BURMA AND INDIA

The tiger probably entered Burma in the course of the last ice age, but as late as the beginning of this century certain villages were considered 'tiger villages' and all the inhabitants were supposedly able to turn into tigers. The tiger has therefore been deeply ingrained in Burmese belief for tens of thousands of years, although the depredations of British colonists and recent Burmese politics have meant that large parts of the forest have been wiped out and if there are any tigers left, they are unknown to the outside world.

A legend from Nagaland in north-eastern India relates that the mother of the first spirit, the first tiger and the first man came out of the earth through a pangolin's den. Man and the tiger are seen as brothers, one in human shape, the other striped. One stayed at home while the other went to live in the forest, but one day they met in the forest and were forced to fight. The man tricked the tiger into crossing a river and then killed it with a poisoned dart. The tiger's body floated downstream, where it was caught in reeds. The god Dingu-Aneni saw that the bones had come from a human womb and sat on them for ten years; as a result, hundreds of tigers were born, some of whom went to live in the hills and others on the plains.

This legend is typical of the belief that tigers and man are closely connected, being born of the same mother. The concept of the 'tigerness' of man the and 'humanness' of the tiger recurs again and again throughout the vast tracts of land where the tiger has roamed. Much of Naga ritual has come down to us from early anthropologists and colonialists who visited the region after the turn of the century, by which time

A Naga chieftain wears a necklace of tiger teeth to guard against evil and to bring him power and courage.

great changes had already taken place in the complicated relationship between the tiger and man, especially as a result of the massive slaughter of tigers that took place throughout the Indian subcontinent in the nineteenth century. Even so, Naga folklore is rich in examples of how the tiger was invoked as a guardian of the area, who would allow men and women to copulate successfully, bringing forth 'seed and fruit'.

Oaths were always taken over a tiger's tooth or skull. As elsewhere, shamans invoked tiger spirits to cure illness. Tales of were-tigers were common: there were many instances in which a tiger was shot or hurt and a man in a nearby village would suddenly find himself with the same injury. The Nagas knew of many 'tiger men' who would reveal a variety of scars on their bodies which corresponded to wounds on 'their' tigers. The effect on these people of non-stop hunting on the part of the British, injuring thousands of tigers, does not bear thinking about.

The Nagas themselves only killed tigers on ritual or ceremonial occasions and even then did not boast of it – 'The village killed a tiger' was the expression they used. Strict taboos governed the cutting, skinning and eating of a tiger's flesh, and in some areas the head would be put in a stream of water so that the spirit would not seek revenge. Alternatively, the mouth might be propped open to allow the spirit to escape. This prevented the tiger god in his wrath avenging himself on the one who had killed the tiger.

The Lhota Nagas put leaves in the tiger's mouth for the same purpose. The Lephori kept tigers' heads in trees and used them in the rituals of oath-taking. A man would take some of his own hair and a bit of earth, place it on the tooth or skull of a tiger and in the open air, between sky and earth, take his oath.

The concept of the eclipse was explained as an attempt by the tiger to eat the moon or the sun, but it could be stopped by the loud playing of drums. It is extraordinary what wide-ranging powers were credited to the tiger.

Spreading down from this north-eastern corner, the tiger's territory extended throughout India, including mangrove swamps, evergreen forests and dry deciduous forests, scaling heights of nearly 2,000 metres in Kashmir and tolerating an incredible variety of temperature and climate. During the nineteenth century there were at least 50,000 tigers roaming India, and there may have been as many as 80,000.

The earliest images of the tiger in India appear on the famous Harappan seals, which survive from the Indus Valley civilization and date from about 2500 BC. These images are sometimes figures of which the front half is a woman and the hind half a tiger. One seal shows the naked figure of a woman, upside down with her legs apart and two tigers standing to one side. The implication is that the tiger is closely connected with fertility and birth and that man and tiger evolved together from the same 'earth mother'. As one expert, Pupul Jayakar, expressed it, 'The earth is the great yoni. The woman's body in the Indus Valley seal is the earthbound root, the fecundating source. The arms of the inverted figure are stretched to touch the knees as in the

Yogasanas (yoga postures). The rampant tigers, guardians of initiation, protect the mysteries and the immense magic of creation.'

One of the most fascinating living cultures that still practises tiger worship is that of the Warlis, a group of tribes living north of Bombay. They live by subsistence agriculture using 'slash and burn' methods and avoiding fertilizers, since they believe that the earth has her own method of fertilizing herself and that manmade fertilizers may render her barren. Like so many other peoples in India, the Warlis' relationship with nature continues even today to encompass a certain amount of giving and taking without over-exploitation.

They live in rugged ranges and foothills which keep them at a certain distance from the outside world. They are known chiefly for their skill in painting, and for their use of geometrical shapes which can be traced back to the earliest rock paintings of Central India, dating from about 3000 BC. They were probably the first people in India to represent images of nature on rock, showing the earth as a mother and endless provider of all things. Warli paintings are often daubed with red as a sign of sanctity: they show the tiger as a natural part of life, sitting or walking through the village with a harmless, friendly look – very much as an undisturbed tiger would appear in reality.

In the course of their history the Warlis have faced Hindu, Muslim, Portuguese, Maratha and British rule, each successive regime being less sympathetic to their way of life. This culminated in 1841 with the British forbidding the Warlis to use the wood of the forest, which was instead given over to the construction of railway sleepers. Nonetheless, much of the Warlis' traditional culture has survived.

They have always believed in the tiger god, Vaghadeva – there are carved wooden statues of the tiger all over their area, many of them phallic symbols reflecting the tiger's importance as the bringer of fertility. Various gods are propitiated in different seasons, with offerings to Vaghadeva being made soon after each harvest, at the time of the New Year festival of Diwali, when the emphasis is on prosperity.

A statue of Vaghadeva is found on all village boundaries and links the various tribes of the area. Just before and during Diwali, when the earth is producing new plants in the harvested fields, the young people sing and dance in a trancelike state to the music of a phallic-shaped instrument called the *tarpa*; when the dancing is over they worship Vaghadeva, commemorating the most productive period of the year for both the earth and the people. It has been said that 'the dancers merged with the darkness, soft, damp and sensuous, and only the stamp of dancing feet could be heard. At last they were free, unwatched, lost in oblivion in the very womb of nature itself.'

This celebration lasts three days and nights. Members of the village donate part of the profits from their harvests to propitiate the tiger, whose statue is adorned with images of the sun, moon, stars and trees, and possibly an entwined serpent – all symbols of life and its endless regeneration.

The gods who look after the fields and the villages are heroic ancestor gods whose task it is to ward off evil, protect the fields and increase fertility for the crops. The installation of these figures as guardians of the village is carried out with great ritual by the *utare bhagats*, priests or medicine men representing the tiger god.

The *utare bhagat* invokes the spirit of the tiger god for healing purposes. Deforestation has limited his role, since he is no longer able to find all the herbs traditionally used in medicine. The name *bhagat* may well be connected with *baghaut*, meaning 'the man who is actually a tiger'. When the *bhagat* goes into a trance, the most important spirit that possesses him is the tiger god, symbolizing all that is powerful and guarding the village from danger and its cattle from attack. At the time of worship, the tiger appears in the nearby forest and watches the rituals from the shade of a tree. In accordance with tribal tradition, no one leaves home on a journey without asking the tiger to protect his village or to solve any problems that might arise. The Warlis regard the tiger as 'the greatest of all gods. The others are there because of him.'

Vaghadeva, who is also known as Vaghya or Gamadeva, is worshipped after the harvest before threshing can begin. Only then will the household gods and the corn mother be propitiated. Although less important than the tiger, the corn mother is particularly significant, as the tiger is regarded as her vehicle. On a seventeenth century silver amulet found in Maharashtra, she is shown riding a tiger. Her body is formed of a leaf and merges with the striped leaves that make up the tiger. The arms of the goddess extend like branches from the trunk of her body, symbolizing the fusion of man, animal and nature.

The tiger's connection with fertility extends even to marriage and pregnancy. A bridal couple wear red and yellow shawls resembling the skin of the tiger; draped in these shawls they visit the temple to propitiate Palaghata, the goddess of marriage. If she is angry, the shawls will turn into a real tiger and devour the couple. If this does not happen, the process sanctifies the couple and renders them fertile for the future.

The tiger god is also the companion of Palaghata and is the first spirit to be invoked during a wedding ceremony. After due deference has been shown to the family gods, the marriage is completed by further worship of the tiger god. The umbar tree plays a vital part in a wedding – tree and tiger have to be married before the couple can be united, and it is the wood of the umbar which covers the couple during the ceremony. The colours red (representing blood), yellow (corn) and white (rice) are used as symbols of fertility and are linked to the colours of the tiger, underlining yet again its involvement with every facet of life, the earth and its productivity.

Various Rajput groups claim descent from the tiger and will never harm it. Many other forest communities worship the tiger as lord of the jungle, while at Petri in Berar there is a special altar to Waghai Devi, the tiger goddess. Legend has it that a woman of the Gond people was seized by a tiger and then vanished completely; since then the altar to the tiger goddess has received frequent offerings.

An altar was often erected on the spot where a tiger had killed a man. The shrine was in the charge of a *baiga* or priest who would light lamps and make offerings of cocks or pigs. Passers-by would throw stones at the altar as a way of laying the man's ghost to rest and keeping the tiger calm – otherwise the dead man's spirit would walk and the tiger would become ferocious. The Gonds built images of the tiger in mud and stone anywhere a tiger had killed one of them. Offerings were then given to these images in the hope of dissuading the tiger from making further attacks.

Tiger images and legends occur throughout Hindu-dominated areas. The god Ayyappa, one of the most popular deities in Kerala in south-western India, represents an ideal who may be approached by all men, whatever their caste or faith, and before whom all find

Five tigers with a single head, from an album of watercolours made in Madras in 1785 and mostly illustrating native peoples and their way of life. The significance of the tigers uniting into one head is not clear, but the presence of tigers in a book about daily life shows that the tiger was an intrinsic part of traditional cultures.

A Warli painting. The striped figure in the centre represents the tiger, the focal point of all their activities and rituals. The style of these modern paintings may have their origins in the oldest rock engravings found in India.

themselves equal, regardless of their background or status. He is the offspring of a brief union between the beautiful enchantress Mohini and the god Shiva. The godling was then left on the banks of the Pampa river in Kerala, to be found by the childless king of Pandalam. Seeing Ayyappa as the answer to his prayers, the king took the child back to his queen and together they reared him as their son.

All went well until the queen unexpectedly gave birth to a son of her own and became insanely jealous of the young boy her husband had found in the forest and declared his heir. She plotted with the chief minister of the kingdom to get rid of Ayyappa: they agreed that the queen would feign a serious illness which could be cured only by drinking tiger's milk, knowing that Ayyappa would offer to obtain the milk for her and would be killed.

The first part of the plot went smoothly and Ayyappa set forth on his mission. However, neither the king nor the queen knew that the reason for Ayyappa's creation was to kill the demon Mahishi and that the time had come for him to perform this task. No sooner had Ayyappa entered the forest than he met Mahishi and, after a great battle, killed her.

Meanwhile, the king, unaware of his wife's plot, waited anxiously for his son's return. When word came that Ayyappa had been sighted, he rushed to greet him and saw that he was riding on a great she-tiger, accompanied by her cubs and carrying a vessel containing her milk. Instantly recognizing the boy's divinity, the king prostrated himself, while the queen, humbled and repentant, begged forgiveness. The royal couple implored the god to stay with them but, his mission on earth accomplished, he had to leave – although he promised he would always protect their kingdom and his devotees.

The pilgrimage to Ayyappa's temple is an arduous one, undertaken after a forty-one-day penance. His followers – mostly men, for Ayyappa is a celibate god and women are not allowed to approach him during their fertile years – have to trek for many kilometres along rough paths through thick jungle, recalling the god's journey to collect the tiger's milk. The pilgrimage is said to be symbolic of the soul's journey to unite with the Supreme Absolute.

A story of a compassionate prince giving his body to save a starving tigress and her cubs is told with variations in several Buddhist texts. According to one version, the young prince Mahasattva was walking over the hills with his brothers when they saw, near the foot of a precipice, a tigress with two cubs. The tigress was little more than a skeleton, and so mad with hunger that she was about to eat her young. Seeing this, Prince Mahasattva left his brothers and, desirous of saving the animals' lives, threw himself down the precipice and lay still, waiting for the tigress to eat him. But she was too weak and exhausted even to bite. So he pricked himself with a sharp thorn to draw blood. By licking the blood, the tigress gained enough strength to devour the prince, leaving only his bones. When his parents found these, they had them buried and raised a mound above the grave. Prince Mahasattva was then revealed to be the Buddha as a *bodhisattva* – one of the numerous preparatory stages of existence through which he passed before emerging as 'the Enlightened One'. It is significant that the story is treated as fact rather than legend in the Buddhist texts: the spot where it is said to have happened is revered and commemorated by a *stupa* or shrine.

In one part of northern Bengal the tiger god was worshipped by both Hindus and Muslims. Scroll paintings depicted the Muslim holy man astride a tiger, carrying a string of prayer beads and a staff and attacking all that was evil.

As elsewhere, it is the mixture of awe for the power of the tiger and the symbolic magic with which it is invested that determines the relationship between man and tiger in many parts of India. In addition, the tiger's role as an agent of fertility was paramount in societies where the produce of the earth and the labour of men and women determined survival more or less on a one-to-one basis.

In one story, a man and woman were in the jungle. The presence of a man called Asur Dano stopped them from making love. Many days passed and the woman thought, 'What shall we do? This Asur has stopped all the joy of our life.' She took a branch from an ebony tree, cut off a lot of little bits and threw them at the Asur; they turned into bears and chased him. She then threw shavings of the saleh tree at him and they turned into tigers. She said to them, 'Go and guard our camp. Do not let the Asur

This detail of a Bengali scroll painting dates from about 1800 and depicts the tiger's association with 'the feminine' and with fertility and reproduction.

near us.' The bears, hyenas and tigers prowled round the camp, keeping the Asur away. The man and woman copulated and there was seed and fruit.

Probably the most widespread belief of all about the tiger concerns its role as Durga's vehicle, a concept that is another relic of the ancient Indus Valley civilization. The image of the tiger as a vehicle has parallels in Siberia, where the tiger spirit (a woman) appears in the form of a winged tiger during the initiation of a shaman; in China, where the founder of Taoism rides on a tiger in his quest for eternal life and his endless battles with demons; and in Tibet, where frescoes depict goddesses riding tigers. But it is in association with Durga that the tiger is at his most powerful.

Durga is the supreme goddess who can bring light to the earth, a force for peace amid the powers of evil. She is in fact the feminine force or *sakti* created by the gods

*T*he goddess Durga astride a tiger, fighting the demons of the world in order to bring new life to earth and defeat the instruments of death. In combination with the tiger, she is unbeatable.

This painting is from Rajastan and dates from about 1800.

to combat the evil male power that had percolated through the world; the name Durga means 'beyond reach'. From her sprang the goddess Kali to join the fight, and the vehicle for this fight was the tiger. Why? Perhaps because tiger and man were deemed to have been born from the same mother, so the tiger was seen as man's sibling, but also as the king of the forest, a power on earth that was 'beyond reach' of any mortal.

Durga relies on the tiger to guide her through the million obstacles on the battle-field of her perpetual fight against evil. In addition, the tiger himself has the strength to attack demons around him. Both goddess and tiger derive their strength from the earth mother and in combination are the most powerful possible force against evil. Without one or the other, the battle might be lost. The tiger, as a manifestation of 'mother earth', is the only possible vehicle for Durga. Even today, the image of Durga riding her tiger is plastered across every corner of India.

A Frenchman travelling in Bengal during the eighteenth century wrote a vivid description of an area steeped in tiger worship. Some of the Bengal tigers were as large as oxen, 'so eager and ferocious in pursuit of their prey that they have been known to throw themselves into the water and swim to attack boats on the river. Notwithstanding the superiority which these creatures possess over human beings by their strength, ferocity and the arms with which nature has supplied them, a certain instinct seems to tell them that men by their intellectual faculties are still more formidable than they; hence they avoid inhabited and cultivated places; or if they sometimes visit them it is only when compelled by hunger.

'But between this place and the Clive Islands they are so numerous that they are sometimes seen in troops on the banks; these islands have been lately brought into a state of improvement for the cultivation of sugar. The clearing of the ground was attended with the loss of a great number of Indians, who were destroyed by these ferocious animals; for, in cutting down the wood with which the face of the country was covered, they were disturbed in their retreats and rushed upon the labourers. What will appear extraordinary, these men never attempted to defend themselves, though their number sometimes amounted to 500.'

This is one of the most vivid records of the beginnings of large-scale agriculture and the destruction of the forests. But how could 'these men' defend themselves when they were forced to destroy the home of their god and in turn the god himself? Since the local communities believed that the tiger was the guardian of the forest, who had control over every tree, they also accepted that the felling of forests provoked the tiger into a raging fury and simply sacrificed themselves to him. Who could deny the tiger's right to protect his forest?

During the period of British rule, innumerable tigers, mostly yellow but also a few white and a few black, were sought out and killed, very largely for sport. One particularly memorable account is worth recording here: the hunter is perched in a tree, waiting to shoot a man-eating tiger near the corpse of its victim:

'I do not think I could have borne the gruesome sight much longer, when there was a roar and a brindled mass sprang at something which was invisible to me. Instantaneously, a vast speckled body coiled itself round the brindled matter, there was a struggle, bones seemed to be crunched to bits, the tiger gave a feeble roar or two, and then all was still except an occasional convulsive heaving.... That long, long night at length terminated and thankful I was to see the dawn of day and hear the jungle fowls proclaim that sunrise was at hand. Losing no time, I descended to solve last night's mystery. The sight that met my eyes was marvellous. A huge rock snake, a python, just over twenty-one feet in length, lay coiled round the body of the tiger whose fangs in turn were imbedded in the back of the snake's head, while the reptile's folds, after enveloping the tiger, had got a purchase by lashing its tail round the adjoining sapling, and so assisted the vast muscular power it possessed in crushing the tiger to death.

'Having procured coolies, with the united strength of twenty men, aided with coils of strong rope, we unwound the snake from its hold on the tree, when a cart being procured, the two, lying dead in each other's embrace, were conveyed to the village.'

It is tempting to speculate on what might have happened if the British had not shot tigers or used their guns against the forest. Would there have been less man-eating? How many tigers roamed the forests with searing bullet injuries, driven to acts of unprovoked aggression through pain and desperation? But whatever might have happened, the fact remains that with the departure of the British, Indian politicians accelerated the process of slaughtering the tiger and destroying the forests with policies of exploitation on a scale that took no account of other needs. It was as if they had decided this was the way to grow rich overnight. How the forests of India must have trembled and quaked in agony as they were bled and destroyed.

Over the last few centuries, killing a tiger has been seen as a symbol of manhood for some of those who ruled India, and countless important people have roamed the forests trying to prove themselves. I have been through records which show that at least 20,000 tigers were shot between 1860 and 1960.

In post-independence India, the forest communities underwent rapid changes as 'modern policy measures' were imposed on their integrated lives. New generations grew up with distorted, confused and anarchic values as the pressures of the developed world disrupted earlier systems of knowledge and belief. In an endless race for riches, little thought was spared for the repercussions. In 1970, the tigers of India were a lost species. By the time a ban on hunting was imposed, there were perhaps 1,800 tigers left – at the turn of the century there had been 40–50,000. In the meantime, the forests had dwindled and the human population increased astronomically; the rich grew richer and the poor poorer.

For the people who lived under the umbrella of the forest, the tiger was the most important, most powerful representation of nature that walked the earth. Nature was the giver of life and the tiger seemed to symbolize the force that could provide

In the state of Kerala in southern India, the manifestation of the goddess Kali in tiger form is celebrated with ritual dancing. Here a male devotee dresses up as the tiger god Vageswani.

life, defeat evil and act as an 'elder brother' to man, defending crops and driving out unhealthy spirits. It was the protector, the guardian, the intermediary between heaven and earth.

The tiger evokes myriad images: tigers who carried princesses on their backs; who grew wings in order to travel great distances to cure and heal; who turned white and became part of the Milky Way, keeping a protective eye on the earth and its inhabitants; tigers and dragons who fought to create rain; tigers who guarded their forests against thoughtless woodcutters; who changed into men and back again; tigers who carried people into the next world; who fought evil so that mankind could love and reproduce; tigers linked to man in so many ways, but with a primary purpose of preventing disaster, regenerating life and providing balance, peace and fertility.

All this is irrespective of the fact that tigers sometimes killed people, long before the arrival of the professional hunter. Forest communities accepted the tiger's right to intervene in their lives – that which gave life also had the right to take it away.

This is even more true nowadays when the tiger's home has been ravaged and destroyed. There are frighteningly few tigers left in the world. Belief in their powers lives on, though as the animal itself dies, the beliefs will gradually suffer the same fate. As new technology has turned forest into agricultural land virtually overnight, the traditional cultures of peoples so closely linked with both tiger and forest have been quietly eroded or deliberately smashed.

Let us now take a closer look at one tract of land in India, where the tiger roamed and still roams, as part of a special conservation plan to preserve this magnificent creature.

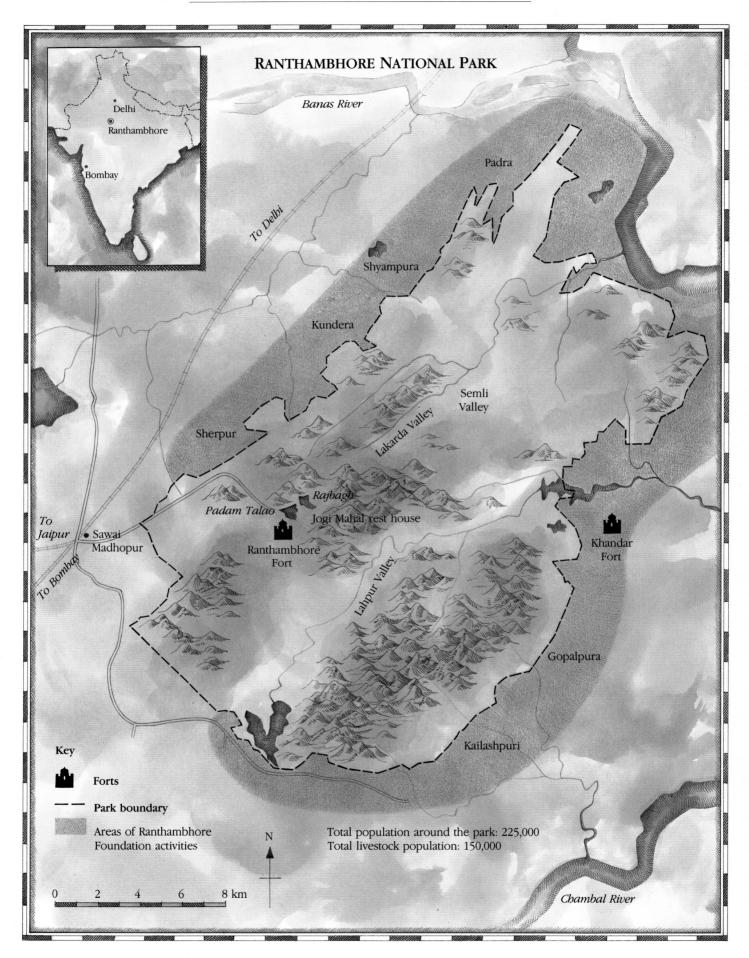

RANTHAMBHORE NATIONAL PARK

Delhi
Ranthambhore
Bombay

Banas River

Padra

Shyampura

Kundera

To Delhi

Semli
Valley

Sherpur

Lakarda Valley

Rajbagh

Padam Talao

Jogi Mahal rest house

Ranthambhore
Fort

Khandar
Fort

*To
Jaipur*

Sawai
Madhopur

Lahpur Valley

To Bombay

Gopalpura

Kailashpuri

Key

Forts

Park boundary

Areas of Ranthambhore
Foundation activities

N

Total population around the park: 225,000
Total livestock population: 150,000

0   2   4   6   8 km

Chambal River

THE
LIFE
OF THE
TIGER

The tigress known as Noon chases a young sambar through water. This unusual behaviour was almost certainly inspired by the example of the male tiger Genghis, the most extraordinary hunter I have seen.

Ranthambhore, in the state of Rajasthan, is one of the smallest of the Project Tiger reserves. Its name comes from the vast fort which stands as a citadel in the middle of the forest. The fort was already in existence in the eleventh century, and the area around it is littered with the ruins of the past: lake palaces, ancient step wells, cupolas, guard posts, temples and memorial stones all bear witness to Ranthambhore's varied and fascinating history.

An eighteenth-century traveller described the fort as being famous throughout India, well protected, completely inaccessible, concealed in mountainous regions where the ridges were high and surrounded the entire fort, leaving only the thick forest gorges below as entrances and exits which could easily be defended. Only cannons could blast through the walls and force entry, and the notorious inaccuracy of cannon fire meant that the fort justified its reputation as unconquerable.

Towers and bastions were built into the wall and into natural rock faces which provided their own special fortifications. The rocks on the edges of the ridges were another disadvantage for any invading army. Only under siege might the occupants of Ranthambhore suffer, but the fort had its own tanks for collecting rain water and twelve villages in the surrounding area to supply food to the garrison.

Today this tract of land where endless battles were fought between warring princes has another ruler: the tiger haunts the narrow gorges on either side of the fort and has even been known to venture atop it!

The life of the nearby town of Sherpur was traditionally closely interwoven with that of the forest. The first changes came in 1925 when a series of dams that had created perennial lakes were broken to make way for 'improved agriculture'. At the time, rice was the principal crop of the area; as water levels fell it gave way to sugar cane and later to wheat and mustard oil. Large areas of the forest around Sherpur were devoted to agriculture. Today everyone in Sherpur village knows that when the lakes of the forest are full, the water table is healthy – a vital piece of information for a way of life that is still influenced by everything that happens in the forest.

The area of the Ranthambhore forest was for centuries controlled by its own chiefs, barely influenced by the changing rulers of the rest of the country. Until the British arrived, they lived freely and easily in the forests. They revered the sun and the moon and were great worshippers of Vaghdeo, the tiger god who was propitiated throughout the forest as lord of the area. They believed in a world of ghosts and spirits and wore a variety of charms and amulets to ward off the evil ones. Even today, some of the villages around Ranthambhore still have a *bhopa* or medicine man. The older generations remember their worship of the tiger and some cattle-herders still ask for the blessing of the tiger god before taking their cattle to graze in the forest. Few people speak the name of the tiger, preferring to use some other term of respect. But the young are changing. Too much has happened too quickly in their lives.

The indigenous residents of the Ranthambhore forests were a people called the Minas. It was their custom to mark the forehead of a new ruler with blood taken from the thumb or toe of a member of a particular family of the tribe. This seems to have been an expression of their right to accept or reject their ruler – as if his subjects were endowing him with power over them as a sign of their allegiance and respect.

Before the arrival of the British, the Minas seem to have lived fairly freely and easily in the forests, but their control over inaccessible trade routes through their land was so strong that they were considered thieves, marauders and murderers by their new masters, who saw them as a thorn in the side of quick prosperity. By 1820 the Rajput and British armies had combined to 'subdue' the jungles and teach these people a lesson. They did this by forming an army corps to recruit as many of the Minas as

*T*he battle of Ranthambhore as depicted in the historical work, the Akbarnama.

they could as soldiers; for the rest, persistent force was used in an effort to make them change their ways.

The Ranthambhore area has always been remarkable for its wildlife. The following description was written in the 1870s:

'In the wooded glens near the Chambal in the south-west, tigers are so numerous that cattle cannot graze in them without special precautions, and the population of the country must be sensibly affected by these destructive beasts. Bears, sambar, nilgai, deer likewise abound in this locality, which would be a paradise for a sportsman. Leaving the Chambal and coming to the uplands of the Dang, game is found wherever there is water. Some of the large tanks only dry up in seasons of extraordinary drought, and these are frequented by tigers, sambars and other game, which during the great famine of 1868 died in great number near the bank.'

By the turn of the century, the Ranthambhore forests had become the private hunting reserves of the Maharajas of Jaipur. In one sense this slowed down the destruction of the forest and the tiger, since only special guests were invited to shoot at an annual one-month camp held in the winter at the edge of Sawai Madhopur, the town just outside what is now Ranthambhore National Park.

Nevertheless, many came. Guests included royalty and nobility from all over Europe, a series of Maharajas and a host of others. Tiger-shooting records were regularly broken here and all over India, but fortunately the shoots in Ranthambhore came under the stewardship of one Colonel Kesari Singh, a man with a remarkable instinctive understanding of the tiger; he managed to satisfy his clients without despoiling the area or allowing the animal populations to be seriously depleted.

Kesari Singh wrote a number of extraordinary descriptions of encounters with tigers. On one occasion, a Mina woman was sitting cooking her food with her children playing around her when a tiger appeared in the enclosure. Without taking any notice of anyone, it walked into the nearest hut. The villagers gathered round and placed a screen of thorns across the entrance to the hut to prevent any 'unforeseen happening'. Kesari Singh was summoned. When he reached the village he made a small hole in the wall of the hut; a strong smell of tiger filtered through, but he saw no sign of life. Then he shone a torch into the darkness and saw the tiger 'sitting up tight in a corner'. There was a deep growl. Kesari Singh shot the tiger through the hole in the wall. On examining it he discovered a series of wounds on its neck, probably caused by a fight with another tiger and now infested with maggots. The tiger had not been able to reach the wounds with his tongue and had been in agony. As Kesari Singh wrote, 'He must have been in fearful distress when he walked, in broad daylight, into a human dwelling – perhaps in some vague way hoping for help and relief.'

On another occasion the conservator of the nearby Nilgiri forests and his assistant were examining a map by the light of a kerosene lamp when a gentle rubbing against the assistant's leg revealed that a tiger had entered the room without their noticing it and had hidden under the table. Astonished and not a little alarmed, the men backed outside and quickly bolted the door. The tiger was shot through a window and, on examination, found to be suffering from festering wounds. Tigers in distress seeking refuge and help from man?

I was witness to a remarkable episode near Sawai Madhopur during the monsoons of 1991. A young male tiger took to leaving the park at night and strolling around the edges of the town, only returning to the security of the forest after sunrise. He was seen on several occasions in the gardens of hotels and offices, and once visited the Project Tiger offices and the homes of the field director and assistant director – as if he were paying a visit to those who were supposed to be protecting him!

One night he entered the compound of the Taj Hotel, lay asleep in the garden for a while and then ambled up the steps and peered in through the front door. He must have had something of a shock, since the hotel has a number of stuffed and mounted tigers and leopards in its lobby.

Early the next morning the tiger was still strolling harmlessly through the town. Police and forest personnel were summoned and found that the tiger had dozed off in the middle of the track that connects Man Town to the old city, bringing the morning office traffic to a halt and gathering a crowd of several hundred people around him. The crowd started chanting slogans at the Forest Department: 'You are cutting the forest, you can't protect the tiger, it's coming to live with us in the town'; 'You made the park so expensive for us local people that the tiger has decided to visit us in our homes.' And so on.

At this moment, the tiger awoke, glanced around and bounded into a nearby field of crops. He was now cut off from the forest with habitation on all sides. The men of the Forest Department had no choice but to tranquillize him and carry him back to the forest, leaving him in a suitable place nearly twenty kilometres away. Fortunately, he awoke nine hours later and wandered off into the night, seeming none the worse for his experiences.

It had been a historic week in the life of the tiger and the residents of Sawai Madhopur.

Much has been written about the ban on hunting and the implementation of Project Tiger in the 1970s. Its effect on Ranthambhore and the surrounding villages is discussed in the final section of this book. For the moment, suffice it to say that it was in 1976 that Ranthambhore entered my life. I knew nothing of its history – I was merely obsessed with the idea of searching for the tiger, and I was privileged to be in this magical place at a time when tigers were more visible than they had ever been before. Very slowly and over a period of sixteen years I have been able to build up a picture of the events that occurred throughout Asia in the land of the tiger – and the horrific changes that have taken place over the last few decades.

It is true that in 'the old days' there were fewer people making demands on the land, and that the claims of modern economics had not impinged on the forest communities. But can it be right that all the primeval forests left in India are now national parks and more like museums than wild places? Can we not look back at traditional wisdom and connect it to the modern world?

This book does not mean to romanticize the past or paint a picture of an idyllic society. It is merely an attempt to understand, assimilate and respect the fine balance that once existed between man, nature and the tiger. The story that unfolds in the following pages is the story of the life and behaviour of the tigers of Ranthambhore, the adaptations they have been forced to make in order to survive and the problems that they face alongside the forest peoples with whom they share their land. The majesty revealed in these pictures may go some way towards explaining why the cult of the tiger came into being.

*I*n the 1970s, the tiger was gasping for life as the pressures on natural resources in India increased dramatically. Becoming completely nocturnal, it was rarely seen in Ranthambhore, or anywhere else in the wild (left).

*H*yena and leopard shared Ranthambhore with the tiger, creeping out at night in their endless quest for food. This hyena (right) had managed to fight off a leopard and appropriate its spotted deer kill.

*I*n the late 1970s, twelve villages that had been located inside Ranthambhore National Park were resettled outside its boundaries, creating a less disturbed environment for the tiger. The sacrifice these people made had a marked effect on the tiger's behaviour: it quickly began to shed its nocturnal cloak, and Ranthambhore was soon famous all over the world for the unusual 'visibility' of its tigers (below).

*W*ater is a vital ingredient in a tiger's life (above). In summer, when temperatures can rise to 47°C, a tiger will spend the day close to a water hole, not only so that it can quench its thirst regularly, but also so that it can position itself strategically when the various prey species come to drink.

*S*oaked in water, it can spend hours cooling off from the effects of the scorching sun, although it always prefers to keep its face out of the water and clear of any risk of splashing (right). It is extraordinary to think that the Siberian tiger survives at temperatures of −20°C or colder in the permanently snow-covered regions of its range.

Whether apparently asleep, fully awake, in water or out of it, the tiger is always alert to the possibility of catching prey, be it deer, antelope or peacock. It can change its mood in a second in order to plan its attack.

*T*he tiger's tongue is vital for health as well as grooming. Its strong, antiseptic saliva minimizes the possibility of infection from a thorn scratch or a wound inflicted by another tiger.

*A*n adult male tiger watches his human observers carefully
as he rests amid a bed of greenery. The tiger spends much
of the day conserving energy, resting, sitting or sleeping. In fact,
an average day may include only a few minutes of hectic activity.

*T*his large, battle-scarred tiger (left) stops the traffic in the middle of a forest road as he surveys the intruders. In Ranthambhore, full-grown males may have a range of up to thirty square kilometres, encompassing the smaller ranges of several females.

A tigress strikes a pose as the first rays of the morning sun glance off her back (right). It is the moment for her to find a day shelter and doze off, probably near a high bank of grass that will serve as camouflage.

A tigress stretches her limbs against a rock below the ramparts of Ranthambhore Fort (below). It is dusk – tiger time – and soon the tigress will be gliding through her range, which might be five to ten square kilometres, patrolling it and searching for prey.

A tigress lifts her head *from a bank of grass near one of Ranthambhore's lakes. This movement means she runs the risk of being seen. As long as she remains still she is practically invisible. It is her choice. The tiger's uncanny use of camouflage is one of the reasons for its success as a hunter.*

A young tiger emerges from a bank of grass in the middle of the day (above). It will probably find somewhere to quench its thirst, change position and hope that some suitable prey will pass nearby. A typically energetic day in the life of a tiger.

This young tiger (right) is about two years old, just starting his solitary adult life after becoming independent from his mother. There is almost certainly already a dominant male in the area – possibly this youngster's father – and the younger tiger must play hide and seek with the older one until he is powerful enough to establish and protect his own range.

A young tiger perched precariously on a rock in late evening. Tigers seem to like high positions from which to look down on possible intruders. If need be they will snarl and grimace to warn off human observers who approach too close.

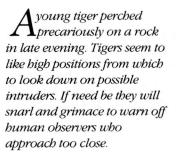

The tiger at its cuddliest. The white of the belly is in sharp contrast to the black and tawny colouring of the rest of the body – it has been suggested that this is because, over the centuries, the belly has had very little sun on it!

*T*his tiger is balanced clumsily near the top of a cliff it is attempting to scale. Adult tigers can weigh 200 kilogrammes, but they are still capable of remarkable feats of agility, scaling four-metre walls and clambering up trees as well as cliffs.

A male tiger's range may encompass a variety of different terrains – open grasslands, plateaux, dry forest and evergreen belts (above). As he walks, he leaves clear indications of his presence, spray-marking or raking his claws on the tree trunks. The freshness of these marks will indicate to another tiger that this territory is spoken for.

P atrolling and defending his territory is an integral part of an adult male's life (right). He can walk long distances while patrolling his range – in Ranthambhore in one twenty-four-hour period he might cover ten to fifteen kilometres.

*T*iger ranges in
Ranthambhore seem to
be clearly defined. I have
often seen a tiger stopping at
a junction, a path or a
certain tree, reversing his
steps as he finds himself
encroaching on another's
territory. These silent means
of communication allow
tigers to avoid conflict – or to
know that they are courting it.

A *male tiger snarls in annoyance (left). The tiger's face can show a wide variety of expressions. During my sixteen years' association with Ranthambhore I must have been charged by tigers at least twenty times, but they were always apparently intending to warn me away rather than to do me serious harm.*

A *n adult male pauses to spray mark the trunk of a tree at the edge of his territory (above). This photograph shows the male tiger's extraordinary ability to reverse his penis between his back legs in order to shoot a jet of fluid on to a chosen spot. The pungent liquid is a mixture of urine and a secretion from the anal gland and the smell can linger for several weeks, proclaiming the tiger's presence.*

Another male smelling the scent may make a 'flehmen' face, in which his face creases up and he lowers his tongue in recognition of the discovery of another tiger in his range. This activity is at its peak after the monsoon, when the rain has washed away all the territorial signs and tigers need to reassert their control of their territories.

*G*reylag geese (right) greet the dawn of a winter's day in Ranthambhore, with the lake and the fort behind it still shrouded in mist. Ranthambhore has nearly 300 species of bird, either resident or migratory. Greylag geese are winter visitors.

A stag party (below). Chital or spotted deer are found in their thousands all over the park and form a vital part of the tiger's diet. Their sharp, carrying alarm call alerts others to the presence of predators in the area – one of the nuances of behaviour that adds to our understanding of the language of the forest.

L *angur monkeys atop the jungle 'flame of the forest' (Butea
monosperma) as it flowers in summer. The langur is the
only primate found in Ranthambhore. Nimble, alert and sharp-
sighted, it fears both tiger and leopard. The sound of its alarm
call from the treetops can be a vital signal for other prey species
– and for human observers trying to trace either predator.*

*W*ild boar and young –
an important part of
the prey base that supports
both tiger and leopard in
Ranthambhore. The adult is a
formidable opponent and
only an experienced tiger is
likely to succeed in killing
one. I once came across a
tiger/wild boar fight outside
the park in the middle of a
village field at night. As I
watched by torchlight, the
boar shrieked and pushed,
managing in the end to force
the tiger away.

*C*lumsily balanced on a treetop, this leopard is the rejected suitor in a complicated courtship ritual. Having found favour with the female concerned, the successful leopard chased his rival up a tree, where he remained in this undignified position for over two hours.

*T*he Indian marsh crocodile (left) infests the lakes and pools of Ranthambhore. Sluggish, shy and cunning, it lives primarily on a diet of fish but can attack small deer – either sambar fawns or adult chital – if they enter the water to drink. Tigers and crocodiles compete for food, and the tiger's superior strength means it usually emerges victorious. Tigers will not only appropriate crocodile kills whenever they can – around the area of the lakes, they have also been known to kill and eat the crocodiles themselves.

*T*he leopard is the most
rarely seen of the
Ranthambhore predators.
Preferring to keep away
from the more powerful tiger,
it spends most of its time on
the cliffs and rocky outcrops.
A tiger will chase a leopard
from its kill and is quite
capable of killing the leopard,
too.

*O*ne of the largest of Asian deer, the sambar (above) is the tiger's most important prey. Its booming alarm call is a sure sign that a tiger is nearby. Ranthambhore is probably one of the finest places in India to see these impressive creatures.

*S*unrise over Ranthambhore's lakes (right). I must have visited this spot hundreds of times, but it is still one of my favourite places – its vistas simply take the breath away.

A tigress lazes at the edge of the lake (above). Tucked in
amongst the trees at the far side of the lake, in the heart of
tiger territory, is the forest rest house, Jogi Mahal. Many visitors
have been surprised by tigresses wandering around the rest house
– one even poked her head into the kitchen.

R anthambhore is a unique mixture of nature and history
(right). Here, a tiger rests in an ancient chatri, part of a
summer palace in centuries gone by. Most of the resident tigers
use this place as a day shelter, walking nonchalantly up its steps
or lounging on its balconies.

A tigress passes in front of the imposing façade of Ranthambhore fort (above), several kilometres in circumference and nearly a thousand years old. Many battles have been fought for control of the fort – now tigers stroll through the ruins.

The relics of a rich past have been taken over not by man but by trees and tigers (right). A tigress sits in the lake of Rajbagh or Garden of the Kings. Behind her is the desolate but beautiful palace which must have been a summer residence of kings in the past.

A tiger yawns at the entrance to a ruined palace (left). I
know of nowhere else in the world where this combination
of tiger, nature and history can be seen.

A tiger paces out of the old arched entrance to a small
palace (above). It is so completely relaxed in these near-
human surroundings that it is no wonder people in many parts
of the tiger's range believed in were-tigers – tigers that could
become men and men that could become tigers.

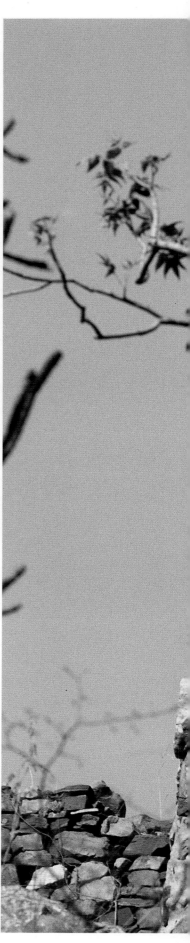

A tigress walks past her favourite day shelter (above) –
one of the abandoned ruins that hint at what the past
must have been like in Ranthambhore.

A tiger stands on the battlements of the fort, looking down
on his kingdom (right). When there were unlimited jungles
across India, the 'corridor' connection and larger tiger
population made for healthier breeding. Now that areas where
tigers can live are so much more restricted and numbers are
so much smaller, inbreeding will inevitably occur; over the next
few decades this will weaken the genetic pool and have an
adverse effect on the species as a whole.

The rains are vital to all life in the forest. In July, the monsoon lashes the forest with incredible force, cascading down the hillsides and rejuvenating the parched land in a matter of days. The forest is like a cup which rapidly fills to overflowing, throwing out gushing rivers to replenish the traditional reservoirs and the underground water-table.

*T*he force of the water is so great that in some parts of the forest it can reach a depth of over two metres, bringing the promise of new life for another year (left).

*T*he forest is quickly transformed as water levels rise, streams gurgle and the sound of water echoes everywhere (right). The colours are lush and plants and animals alike are given the opportunity to grow and to reproduce.

A pair of tigers rest at a water hole. The tigress is in oestrus and her distinctive spray markings and vocalizations have attracted the male. During oestrus a tigress may call for many days in the hope that a male tiger will respond. The male and female will then spend several days together – the only time in an adult tiger's life that this happens.

*M*ating is accompanied by aggressive foreplay – here, the female slaps the male's face (left)! The tigress is the assertive partner, initiating the mating when she chooses. In all my years of watching tigers, I have only ever seen mating once, but it is an experience that remains vividly in my memory.

*W*hen a pair of tigers mate (above), the forest resounds with their roars and snarls. Mating continues at frequent intervals over a period of several days. Aggression alternates with tenderness as the tigers nuzzle and cuddle each other. The tigress repeatedly brushes her flank against the male to encourage him to mate with her. She then crouches receptively. Coitus lasts only fifteen seconds or so, but this pair mated eight times in an hour and a half. Little wonder that various parts of the tiger's body are considered to have aphrodisiac properties and are much sought after in traditional Chinese medicine. The gestation period is between 90 and 110 days, though the tigress remains remarkably slim until the last few days, when the bulge of her belly confirms to the human observer that she is pregnant. If she has not conceived she will come into oestrus again after a few months.

*J*ust before giving birth, the tigress will find a thick area of forest or other secure hiding place for her cubs. Mortality is high at birth: although seven foetuses have been found in a shot tigress, only two or three cubs normally survive the first few days. Ranthambhore has seen instances where four or five cubs have survived, but they are exceptional. In this extremely rare photograph, a tigress gently carries her cub, aged 15–20 days, in her mouth, moving it from one den to another.

This is the moment when tigress and cub are at their most vulnerable, exposed between one refuge and another. Human observers have to be careful to respect the tiger's needs at times like this – approaching slightly too close or accidentally blocking the path between the mother and her cubs might have caused her to attack or alarmed her in such a way as to put her cubs at risk.

A tigress will look after her cubs for two years, during which time she will be totally dedicated to their welfare. Since the cubs are born blind and helpless, the first few weeks are a particularly bitter struggle for survival. The tigress will move her cubs (left) if there is any disturbance in the area around her den – humans, tigers or other predators may all pose a threat.

These photographs show one of the most secret activities in the tiger's life and, to the best of my knowledge, it is the first time it has been photographed. In the course of a morning, the tigress moved her three cubs one by one over a distance of one and a half kilometres, taking them to a safer den (right). Here (below) she returns for the last one, which has boldly emerged from the long grass to meet her.

*A*s the cubs grow, their mother spends a lot of time licking, cleaning, nuzzling and cuddling them (left). She leaves the den to hunt, but remains as close as possible so that she can return at any hint of danger to the cubs. At this time the tigress is fiercely protective – on several occasions forest guards have accidentally encountered one with young cubs and have been furiously charged, forcing them to run for their lives.

A close, warm and loving bond links tigress and cubs into a tightly knit family unit (above). It is a joy to watch the care and affection that obviously exists between them. After being confined to their den for the first month, the cubs are now curious and confident enough to explore the immediate surrounding area – though they keep very close to their mother's side.

The tigress is at her loving best with her cubs (above), apparently so tender and caring that it is tempting to impart human emotions to her. This close physical contact protects the cubs, who at this stage are still very vulnerable and utterly dependent on their mother.

There can be few mothers to match the tigress for devotion (below). I have never heard of a tigress abandoning cubs, nor even of one who was not ever-present for them during the first few months of life.

The tigress is also a firm disciplinarian, giving even very young cubs a clear idea of what they may and may not do (right). Their survival depends on their learning caution and patience. Nonetheless, young cubs spend a lot of time in fun and frolic, rolling and nuzzling each other and their mother.

*W*hen the cubs are a few months old, the tigress will escort them around small areas of her range so that they can absorb details of the terrain around them. These first exploratory days are important for the cubs in learning the language of the forest.

A cub clambers on his mother's back in a burst of exuberance. One of the most touching experiences in watching tigers is to see cubs greeting their mother when she returns from hunting after a prolonged absence. Her arrival provokes much purring, nuzzling, cuddling and rubbing of flanks. I once watched three cubs welcoming their mother home and the four tigers remained completely entangled in ecstasy for half an hour.

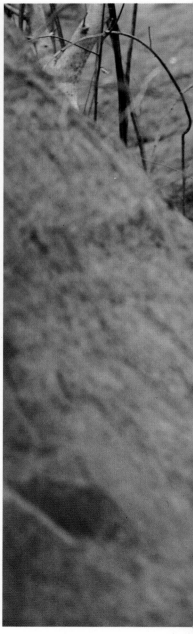

E ven very young cubs can take up aggressive postures in imitation of their mother (right). Here, the dominant cub of a litter, only two months old, makes an effort to protect his den in the tigress's absence.

*A*nother most unusual picture. A tigress sprawls across a track as she suckles her three cubs. At first, their mother's milk provides all the nourishment the cubs require. Their tiny paws push outwards around the tigress's belly to stimulate the flow of milk. After about three months the cubs will also begin to chew at bits of meat that their mother brings back to the den.

A unique picture of tigers in the wild. The adult male who must have fathered the litter has joined the tigress and cubs in a tiny pool of water. The male tiger has always been regarded as a threat to cubs and many instances of young being killed by adult males have been recorded. But in Ranthambhore males sometimes feed on a tigress's kill or allow her and her cubs to share theirs. I have also seen them playing with young cubs. A male tiger's territory usually overlaps the ranges of several tigresses and he may spend short periods with the different females and their cubs.

It seems likely that a male will only kill cubs when he has just taken over a new territory, in order to mate with the resident tigresses and father his own cubs.

*B*y the time the cubs are six months old (above and right), they are growing rapidly and their mother must hunt more and more often to satisfy their increasing appetites. The cubs are now beginning to travel more freely and over longer distances, though they are still accompanied by their mother. They gradually adjust to new sights and sounds, forming a basis of experience that will be vital to their success as adults.

*T*he banks of tall grass that surround Ranthambhore's lakes provide a refuge for the cubs and act as day shelters while their mother scours the lakeside for prey. The cubs will squeak if they are disturbed and a few squeaks will bring the tigress back in a moment to solve her family's problems.

*W*hile the cubs are young, agile and energetic they often
test the strength of their limbs by climbing trees (left); they
may then spend hours resting among the branches. By the time
they become sub-adults they are too heavy for this activity.

A young cub balances on the branch of a tree (above) while
the shadow of the fort rises behind it. Cubs seem to enjoy
chasing each other up trees and raking their sharp claws on the
bark. Like other forms of play, it teaches them to use their strength
and co-ordination in a way that will stand them in good stead
in the future, developing muscles and practising their not very
refined hunting techniques.

*T*wo cubs, now over a year old, explore a pool of water on a misty morning (above). At this age, they have voracious appetites and it must seem to them that most of their lives are spent waiting for their mother to summon them to a kill. Soon they will begin to practise hunting for themselves, stalking peacocks and occasionally inexpertly 'helping' their mother in her own hunting.

*P*lay-fighting is another means of testing strength (left). Cubs spend a lot of time bounding around and jumping on each other with paws stretched outwards.

By the time the cubs are fifteen months old, their play is becoming more aggressive; they swat each other and play rougher games among themselves. The dominant cub, which may be male or female, increasingly asserts itself over the others and a definite hierarchy emerges. The other cubs may roll over on their backs, indicating their submission to the dominant sibling.

A mother and her sub-adult cub late one evening at the edge of a lake. The cub is nearing independence and will soon leave her mother to mark out a territory of her own.

Two cubs completely entangled in an embrace. Their physical closeness diminishes as they grow older and develop individual character traits. All the adult tigers that I have observed have their own distinct 'personalities'.

A *cub leaps playfully on her mother and she responds aggressively. The tigress becomes much less patient with her cubs as they grow up. She is probably exhausted by the need to hunt constantly in order to feed her young – the time is approaching when they must learn to fend for themselves.*

M *other and cubs feed on a sambar kill (left). The carcass is literally torn apart as the hungry sub-adults fill their bellies amid a confusion of legs, hooves and stripes.*

*F*amily life in
Ranthambhore. In the
beautiful light of early
morning, two cubs attack
each other playfully as their
mother watches out for any
sign of danger.

*A*cub plays with a piece of wood, swatting it back and forth with tail raised high (above). I have seen cubs at various stages of growth investigating and playing with unusually shaped objects such as stones and bits of bark.

*A*sub-adult plays with an antler much as we might kick a football (right). Certainly the antler must seem a curious object, whether or not the cub is aware of what once stood below it.

*A*fter a furious battle with half a dozen crocodiles, this tigress has appropriated a sambar carcass and is dragging it away from the lake towards a bank of tall grass (left). Her grown cubs anxiously await their meal – one of them even tugs at her tail as if to make her hurry up.

*Y*oung tigers often rest under the spreading branches and roots of a banyan tree (right). These extraordinary giant trees are common in Ranthambhore and provide refuge and shelter for tigers during the hot summer months.

*M*other and cub emerge from the tall grass. These are the last months of togetherness: solitary adulthood looms for the young tiger, while the tigress will soon come into oestrus again and look for a mate to father her next litter.

A tigress and her cub take an afternoon siesta on a large rock. These rocks are usually surrounded by thick undergrowth and mean the tigers are hidden from any prey that may wander by.

A tigress with three cubs, now nearly eighteen months old. The cubs accompany their mother on hunting expeditions and help her by causing much confusion among the sambar or chital. One cub may chase an animal to one side, another will push it in the opposite direction and suddenly the strategically placed tigress will pounce. Even at this age the cubs are unable to kill on their own.

*T*his may be the last time these sub-adults cuddle like this. But some form of sibling bond seems to last into adulthood. I think that the tigers in Ranthambhore recognize their litter mates and their parents, and sustain kin links.

The cubs still wait anxiously for their mother to return, but they can survive in her absence. The dominant cub in particular shows signs of restlessness and will soon be departing to start a life of his own.

*T*wo sub-adults stroll through the forest. They are still attached to their mother, but have acquired enough confidence to move around the area on their own. Over the last year the tigress has familiarized them with her entire range and they have learned to understand the signals it gives them.

*A*t nearly twenty-two months, this sub-adult is ready to leave mother and siblings (left). The tigress has taught him everything she can. But with increasing human pressure on India's natural resources, even her devoted efforts may not be sufficient to ensure his survival.

*T*hese three cubs are close to independence. They chase partridges, jump on hares, kill peacocks and occasionally even successfully stalk chital fawns. The tigress spends longer periods away from her family and is sometimes absent for a day or two.

*T*igers are often seen strolling along the roads in Ranthambhore (above). This is probably the last walk this mother and cub will take together.

*A*chital is grazing just outside the picture (right). The young tiger has frozen, completely alert, paw raised off the ground. Should he move forward and attack? His mother's training means he knows what to do, but in the first years of independence many attempts at hunting – perhaps ninety-five per cent – will end in failure. But the tiger must hunt to survive and gradually he perfects his skills.

*T*he power behind the paws will one day join forces with the fearsome canines to provide the adult tiger with food.

*S*ome 200 kilogrammes of tiger are concentrated into this mighty spring (right). The sinews of the body ripple like water, fluid and quivering. If the leap falls short it will normally mean the end of the attack – tigers are too heavy for prolonged chases and depend on the power of their initial attack, or on surprise, for most of their hunting successes.

*A*nother young tiger has stalked a chital herd taking cover in the grass. He is poised for attack. At this age, he will almost certainly be unsuccessful, but the moment is charged with excitement as he flexes his powerful muscles.

An experienced tigress struggles to subdue a vast sambar stag. She has taken hold of the cheek rather than the neck, and that unsuccessful grip makes this remarkable picture possible. Otherwise the sambar would be dead. As it is, a battle rages.

The sambar has shaken off the tigress's first assault, but now she has locked into the back of his neck. Although the sambar weighs nearly twice as much as the tigress, he is under great pressure – his hind legs lift involuntarily off the ground.

But the tigress's grip is not strong enough and the sambar breaks free once more. Now the tigress works her way under the sambar and grabs his hind legs. The sambar is still struggling as the tigress does her best to break his leg.

This was an extraordinary example of the strength and determination of an experienced huntress. But still she failed. The sambar escaped by swimming across a nearby stretch of water, nearly drowning from exhaustion after this titanic struggle. The tigress watched him from the bank, too tired to give chase. After a few days of hunger she found and killed another sambar. The sambar she had been struggling with died some weeks later of his wounds.

Nearly ten years ago, Ranthambhore boasted a master predator who had perfected the technique of chasing over quite long distances and killing sambar in water. We called him Genghis (right). His success rate was remarkable – as much as one in eight or even one in five hunting attempts resulted in a kill. I have never known another hunter like him. After he had attacked a wading sambar, he would disappear underwater with it, emerging a few seconds later to carry his kill to dry land.

*G*enghis charges from
cover, taking the
sambar completely by
surprise. Before they had time
to think about running
away, the tiger had singled
out one of the younger
animals as his victim.

*B*efore Genghis, there were few recorded instances of tigers
hunting in water. But Genghis did it frequently, and
constantly came into conflict with the resident crocodiles, from
whom he shamelessly stole kills (left). His example also affected
the behaviour of Noon, the resident tigress of the lakes area. She
also used to chase young sambar in the water and was sometimes
successful, but not nearly as often as Genghis was. While
Genghis was in his prime, Ranthambhore was full of tension and
excitement and no human who saw him has ever forgotten him.

*A*tiger with the carcass of a nilgai or great Indian antelope
*(above). There are two species of antelope in
Ranthambhore, the nilgai and the cinkara or Indian gazelle.
The tiger is known to prey on both.*

*A*tigress straddles the chital she has just killed as she carries
*it away to somewhere she can feed in peace (right). Tigers
are immensely powerful and can carry or drag a carcass that
weighs up to 300 kilogrammes.*

*T*his is a rarely documented activity, unique in my
*experience (below). A tigress chokes a langur monkey to
death. I had watched her sleeping all day, then in the late
afternoon there was a rustle in the grass. A langur approached
and with one pounce she had him pinioned. Within an hour
she had finished eating him. The langur spends most of its time
in trees, where it is completely safe from tiger attack, but on the
ground it is vulnerable.*

The tigers of Ranthambhore remain around a carcass until it is completely consumed, guarding it jealously from vultures or other scavengers. Here, however, the resident male has successfully appropriated a tigress's sambar kill. Tigers are individualistic in their eating habits – some adult males can consume thirty kilogrammes of meat at a sitting; others will chew and nibble at a kill over a period of several days.

A tigress feasting on a male nilgai (left). Once, ten years ago, nine tigers were seen feeding on the same carcass. This has never been seen again, and indeed adult tigers rarely feed together. That memorable meal was presided over by a tigress whom we knew to be related to six of the other tigers present. It was a historic example of communal feeding and provides some evidence that tigers continue to tolerate their relatives after the cubs have become independent.

Two young adults tear a chital carcass apart (right). On the rare occasions when tigers do feed together, it is amidst a cacophony of growls, snarls and grunts as they fight for the spoils.

*T*his tiger must be an experienced hunter – it has succeeded in killing a large male wild boar. The male's tusks usually enable it to put up a tremendous fight and the tiger often walks away hungry from such an encounter.

A tigress eating a peacock. Watching a tiger chasing one of these spectacular birds is an amazing sight, but this is a small meal for a full-grown tiger: the bird is plucked and eaten rapidly and the tiger will soon have to hunt again. Young tigers stalk peafowl as part of their first forays into hunting for themselves – they serve as an hors d'oeuvre on the tiger's menu. After a substantial meal the tiger's belly is so overloaded that it can appear nearly double its normal size.

*A*tigress carries off the remains of her kill. But she may not be allowed to eat it undisturbed. Crows, vultures, tree pies and shrieking jackals may all try to interfere. They also attract still more unwelcome attention. Human observers can track down tigers by following hovering vultures and diving crows. So can other tigers.

*A*tigress senses a threat to her kill (right). She is alert, the atmosphere is charged. In the distance, an adult male – probably a transient in the area – is quietly sniffing his way towards the female. She becomes aware of him and slips into the long grass.

*T*his young tiger picks at the remains of a carcass, cleaning off every scrap of meat (below). He is too young to be an expert hunter and it may be some time before he kills again.

*The unknown male
approaches the tigress
and they face each other,
crouching, snarling and
grimacing. There is no way to
avoid confrontation and
soon they leap towards each
other, balancing on their
hind legs.*

*The tigress lashes out with
her left paw, punching
the male in the face (below).
But she is no match for his
superior size and strength –
she soon rolls over in a
gesture of submission while
the male steals her kill. She
can only watch him feed
from a distance.*

*This young tigress has been badly injured by another tiger
as she tried to defend her kill (above). It took a month for
the wound to heal, during which time she licked it continually,
covering it with the antiseptic of her saliva to prevent infection.
Conflicts over feeding rights can be serious, especially when
prey is in short supply. As the pressures on Ranthambhore grow,
this will happen more often – and tigers can be fatally injured
in such fights. But the alternatives are not attractive – either the
tigers will starve, or they will be forced to leave the park and
hunt in unknown and unprotected areas.*

*In June 1992 I was involved in an official tiger census in which
the tigers of Ranthambhore National Park were counted over a
period of eight days. The estimated population could be as low
as 15–20 animals. There is a severe problem with the tigers of
Ranthambhore, and those that live there have changed their
behaviour, becoming shy, evasive and nocturnal, much as they
were when Project Tiger started.*

*A young tiger moves stealthily forward, poised to attack if
necessary. Even from behind, it gives an impression of the power
that has made it one of the world's most awesome predators.
We cannot allow it to perish.*

THE
TIGER'S
DESTINY

The pressures of politics are enormous in India. This artist's impression of degraded forest is a frightening reminder of the ever-increasing threat to the tiger's realm.

The marked change in tiger behaviour in Ranthambhore which made it possible to take many of the photographs in the preceding section came about because twelve villages within the forest were moved to areas outside the forest in 1976–1979. The idea was that the tigers would suffer less disturbance if the resident human population were removed. Ranthambhore was by this time a protected area, a Project Tiger reserve, although it did not attain national park status until 1981.

About a thousand people were involved in the resettlement. At the time, India was under emergency rule and the government was all-powerful, neither answerable to a constitution nor concerned with human rights or dignity. For the villagers it was a time of fear and trauma and although in theory they agreed to be resettled, in reality they had little choice in the matter. They sacrificed their traditional way of life in the interests of the tiger – and have since suffered from persistent alienation and isolation, rather than receiving the accolades they deserve for their services to conservation.

All sorts of new expectations have been imposed on them and the people who were already living around the park. They have to maximize agricultural production, generate income, cope with a new education system, regreen the areas around them, develop modern scientific attitudes and move as quickly as possible from bullocks and carts to tractors and trucks. Either they adapt or they are abandoned to struggle on as best they can.

In order to attempt to understand the problem, let us look briefly at the fragile ecological system of Ranthambhore and the history of the people and the forest. The first European travellers arrived in Ranthambhore during the latter part of the seventeenth century. Before this, despite the many battles and changes in rulers, the area seems to have survived more or less intact and the variations in its rhythms were gradual and gentle. The village communities were hunter-gatherers or subsistence farmers, part of a feudal system in which they owed allegiance to a clearly defined series of overlords, maharajas and princes. These rulers in turn were expected to take a patriarchal concern in the well-being of their subjects – and that included the well-being of the forest. The British disapproved of the tradition of anointing a new maharaja with the blood from one of his subjects' toes – and with the wiping out of this symbolic gesture, a vital link between the forest communities and those who ruled them was broken.

From the beginning of the nineteenth century, increasing interaction with the Rajput rulers and the British East India Company seems to have stirred up the area: natural resources were exploited faster and the forest people were forced to change their ways, skills and sources of income as they became subservient to an alien system. Many of them were inducted as soldiers; others were pushed into agrarian economies. The rulers' priority was to make routes through the forest safe so that commerce could flourish.

Intensive farming of cotton and indigo was introduced in order to supply essential raw materials to the burgeoning British textile industry. Forests were felled to clear the way for the new plantations and to provide wood to build ships in order that the British navy could

A miniature painting from the renowned Kotah school in India, showing a tiger hunt and the many ways in which the tiger faced death. Hunters took a vast toll on the tiger population the world over.

patrol and protect its vast Empire. As railways expanded, more wood was needed for sleepers and as fuel for the locomotives. An increased demand for paper, which had previously been made from non-wood materials, was suddenly also a drain on the forests. (It is encouraging to note that there is one family in Sawai Madhopur which still carries on the tradition of handmade paper using recycled non-wood material such as fibre and jute.)

The management of such basic commodities as water and salt was taken out of the hands of the forest people. The upshot of these changes was that the system people understood was thrust aside and they were forced to submit to new masters who took no account of their culture, and had no respect for their traditional way of life.

The forests' role in maintaining an ecological balance in soil and water conservation was widely recognized by local communities, who were careful not to let their own needs draw too heavily on these precious resources. But when the British created 'reserved forests' and vast quantities of teak from the Western Ghat Mountains, sal from central India and conifers from the Himalayas were felled to meet the needs of the Empire, complex links of traditional ecology in the villages were broken. Over a period of years, not only timber but medicinal plants, fuel, fibre and oils became scarcer, forcing changes in the lives of the people. Nature was such an integral part of their culture that denying them access to the forests must have had a disturbing emotional effect in addition to the practical problems it imposed.

Having turned the forests 'commercial', the British now instituted a programme of replacing indigenous trees with more convenient, introduced species – with a devastating effect on the underground water-tables all over India. Scientists and forest-dwellers alike are aware of the link between forest and water, but the wisdom of the forest-dwellers can reveal facets of water conservation of which even the experts are ignorant. They know the traditional reservoirs of an area, they know what effect their being full has on the underground water, and they know where there are dams that might need reinforcing in order to replenish the water-table.

Other traditional skills also faded as the native peoples were denied access to the forests. Taking lacquer from the chila tree and using it to make jewellery and other decorative objects, and extracting the essence of khas grass to make Indian perfume were both established sources of income generation in Ranthambhore which had to be abandoned. Tradition and modern ways came into severe conflict as the latter imposed a 'new cultural order', dependent on rapid development for the acquisition of material wealth. The wisdom of generations was torn apart as civilization spread its tentacles across the world – and that wisdom, once destroyed, could never be replaced. Nobody seemed to consider that when human beings lose their past, their future is also endangered.

The 'land of the tiger' faces similar onslaughts throughout Asia. Only tiny populations survive in Siberia and China; in Vietnam, Thailand, Bangladesh, Malaysia and Sumatra forests are being destroyed because of the need for timber, vast tracts of land are needed for agriculture, and poaching is an ever-present threat. The problems of Ranthambhore reflect the worldwide tiger crisis.

Long before India attained independence from the British, Mahatma Gandhi said, 'It is a charge against India that her people are so uncivilized, ignorant and stolid, that it is not possible to induce them to adopt any changes. It is a charge really against our strength. What we have tested and found true on the anvil of experience, we dare not change. Many thrust their advice upon India, but she remains steady. This is her beauty. It is the sheet anchor of our hope.' Today it is still true that people in the remotest parts of India resist change and cling on to their traditional rhythms of life whenever they can.

In the period leading up to independence, Gandhi was able to draw on this reluctance to accept change to encourage people to rise up against the British. The Indians' belief in the superiority of their own ways – whether it concerned the village, agriculture, skills, cottage industry or the right of every human being to respect, whatever his religion or caste – was instrumental in their opposing the colonial system and eventually forcing the British to leave.

What emerged after independence was a mess. Gandhi was assassinated and it fell to Nehru to guide India through its first decades of freedom. Despite the complications of the moment, the country breathed a sigh of relief, as if the worst were over. But India had been propelled into freedom carrying the combined burden of its caste system, its deeply ingrained feudal values, the residue of a colonial administration and the effects of a world that was developing rapidly all around it. The constitution of a free India envisaged equality for each individual within a democratic, socialist framework. However, intentions proved to be one thing and practice another.

The administrative system that was carried forward after independence divided the country into districts. Each district has an administration whose responsibilities encompass land, revenue, forests, agriculture, rural development, income generation, energy systems, water conservation, education and, of course, law and order. A district is run by a district magistrate or collector who is a civil servant, appointed by the politically elected leader of the state government. The collector does not represent a party and is supposed to be non-political.

For each area of activity within a district there is an administrative head who is answerable to the collector, who in turn is answerable to senior civil servants in the state capital. Central government in New Delhi allocates resources according to five-year plans and advises the state government on what to do. But the state government has the final power over implementing policies and administering its territory. Both central and state governments are democratically elected, though they are separate entities and may have different political parties in the majority.

This is the basis of India's federal structure, a system which envisaged a delegation of authority whereby the civil servant would remain non-political and the politician non-interfering. But in fact the British left behind a melting pot in which everything was less clear cut in reality than it seemed on paper, and over the years it became apparent that the roles of civil servants and politicians were frequently fused together in an endless cycle of doing each other favours and creating citadels of power for themselves, often at the cost of the best interests of the people.

Traditional wisdom and knowledge were discarded in the hope of achieving rapid development. There was little genuine assimilation of the cultural heritage of native peoples or forest communities; indeed, the administration had so little understanding of the people that it introduced a system of 'scheduled' or 'reserved' castes, reflecting government's attitude to these people, an attitude rooted in the history of India which now more than ever reasserts artificial differences between people. These groups were officially designated as 'backward' and therefore became entitled to grants, loans and various forms of positive discrimination which reinforced imagined distinctions between sections of the population. Eighty per cent of the people in the Ranthambhore area are Minas and are 'scheduled'. This whole concept reflects the constant negation of all that is traditional, indigenous and ingrained in the spirit of the people. It continues the process introduced in colonial times of judging good and bad without having the humility to absorb the essence of an unfamiliar culture.

In the decades following independence, the village peoples watched changes taking place at a rapid rate as technology advanced. The plague of consumerism that infected the rest of the world to the detriment of environmental awareness made itself felt in India, too. The introduction of television overturned values that had been established for centuries. A villager from Ranthambhore sums up the feelings of his generation:

'We as adults are not flexible any more. We have seen levels of abuse and alienation that you cannot begin to imagine. It is difficult to trust anyone or to believe in the future. Our children will lead the future. But we are worried. At the moment they only sing songs taken from advertising films, they watch television. We see someone on television having a bath, or cars and tyres falling from the sky, or people living in houses with kitchens we could never dream of. We see those strange serials about the rich, showing the absurd lives they lead. And we keep watching this new kind of entertainment, especially the children, who are hypnotized by it. But it changes life.

'What will our children find to do in the future? The schools give no education. The children get nothing from history, maths, science. They are no longer interested in cows, buffaloes, trees, water, milk, agriculture or any traditional skill that used to provide an income. Why can't the schools teach them these skills so that there is a chance for them to earn an income round the village – if they leave for the city it will be the end. The only hope for the future is that they work here, live here, make the area fertile and green.

'If you want the forest to live, the village to grow, the tiger to survive – so do we. But change the schools' approach, change television. Don't influence us with dreams. Let's look at realities and possibilities of developing what we are familiar with and not what is foreign to us. If the children go the way they are going at the moment, nothing will be possible. All that is happening is that they too are rejecting their culture, tradition and way of life – and for what?'

By the early 1970s, India's forests were in grave danger because the few who wanted to 'get rich quick' overwhelmed the vast reservoirs of traditional knowledge. At the end of 1971, a plan to save the tiger was formulated in an office in Switzerland with input from the World Wildlife Fund, as it then was, and the International Union for the Conservation of Nature. In 1973, in a small room in the Ministry of Agriculture in Delhi, it was decided to include Ranthambhore in Project Tiger.

News of the decision was passed on to Jaipur and finally to Sawai Madhopur, where the small forestry office was turned into a Project Tiger office, with all activities in the field becoming their responsibility. But when a new scheme or policy is to be implemented in Ranthambhore National Park, the decision is almost always made in the city, by people with little experience or understanding of the forest.

This is how one Ranthambhore villager recalls the introduction of Project Tiger:

'I was a young man then, with political ambitions. Life was good, much easier than now. The forest spilled over to the edge of our village, the hillsides were carpeted with dhok trees, firewood and fodder were nearby and more than enough for our needs. Our village had less than half its current population, and we grew enough to support ourselves. The rains were always plentiful and we had enough water in our wells, four or five metres below the surface. Because of the rains and the moisture in the soil, we used to manage to harvest two crops a year. Now even one is a problem. Sometimes there was so much water and the soil was so wet we didn't even have to plough the land, we just scattered seeds into this thin layer of water.

'For many generations, through our forefathers, we had known that this forest was our provider, be it in relation to levels of water, wood to cook with or fodder and local fruits. We lived with a traditional knowledge of the ways of the forest. As a boy, I would walk through the forest, along its paths, nallahs and hilltops, sometimes watching deer or the occasional tiger and also collecting what my family and I might need for the day. The forest grew with me as I grew. When we cut wood, we cut those trees whose branches would grow again and we tried never to kill a tree. In fact, most of the wood we collected was from trees that had fallen in storms, wood that was already dead. Cutting down a living tree was a sin and few dared to do it.

'Even in 1973 most of the medicines we used came from the forest – the grasses, the shrubs, the leaves. Different plants and trees had different uses and simple cures were practised by a few respected men in the village. Pastes of leaves, crushed berries, stems of shrubs were part of an infinite knowledge that had been absorbed in the village. We all knew something about it and respected, even feared, what the forest produced and provided.

'I think it was in 1973 that we first heard in the village that a new project was starting to save the forest. We were all interested and excited about this, and there was a lot of discussion about how it would affect us, whether it would be good or bad. Everyone wanted to know more, to talk over the new project with someone in authority, someone who knew what was going on.

'But 1973 turned into 1974 and nobody came to tell us anything. The only way we found out was by quietly watching the restoration and increase in size of the forest post in the village. From having one forest guard who was part of our daily life, with whom we could exchange ideas and share problems, we suddenly had four guards in neat uniforms with curling smiles on their faces that seemed to signal power and confidence. We asked them what was happening. They said wait and see. We waited. Soon a forester sahib was posted to the village to look after the area between the villages of Sherpur and Shampura.

'By the end of 1974, we in the village finally realized what was happening. The realization came early in the winter – a time when we collect and store wood for the cold months ahead. I had gone towards the forest with my friends, to collect dead wood, as I always do. It was early morning – the hill ranges had their usual coat of mist and were carpeted with thick dhok trees. Suddenly we were confronted by the forester sahib and his new forest guard. They held huge sticks in their hands and said, "This is no longer your forest. This is now Project Tiger and legally you cannot cross this line, or collect dead wood or any leaf, grass or anything that grows beyond this line. If you do, we can register a case against you. It is now our forest to protect."

'I was shocked and astounded. The forester sahib had that confident smile on his face. He knew that we depended on the forest, that we had to get wood to cook, simply to survive. Then the guards came up and whispered to me, "Forester sahib will collect wood, but you must give him regular wood. That is his power."'

India had inherited over the centuries an administrative system that swallowed up the individual and became uglier and uglier. Few who entered it could fight it. This is a story of 'the system'.

When Project Tiger was implemented, there was little effective co-ordination between central and state government, little rapport between state government and what was happening 'in the field', and little genuine commitment from those in the field to the area they had to administer and conserve. I think a large part of the problem lies in the 'boss' syndrome – the idea that a politician or senior civil servant can order a junior official to do something, irrespective of whether or not that order is the best way for the junior official to carry out his duties. 'Could you employ the

Huge numbers of livestock feed at the fringe of the national park, destroying precious undergrowth.

following persons in the following jobs?' and 'Could you arrange free transport and meals for these people who are my guests?' are typical requests; 'Could you ensure that even if there are genuine problems concerning grazing or poaching, no one will find out about it?' is more serious. In either case, a junior official would not dare to disobey – a senior civil servant has the power to transfer members of his department at will, and the junior man's whole family could be uprooted as punishment for his so-called insubordination.

I know of forest guards who have worked in the homes of senior politicians in Delhi and Jaipur, providing services for the bosses rather than looking after their posts in the forest. I have seen junior officers in the field who have had to watch their empires being misused by those above them, finding it easier to go along with the corruption rather than fight against it. It is the forest guard at the lowest level of administration who can conveniently become a collector of illegal revenue for his bosses. This revenue comes from the village and the guard can take his percentage before passing it on.

The first possible source of 'supplementary' income for the forest guard is grazing rights – a village can be forced to contribute to the local forest post for the privilege of grazing its herds into the buffer and core zone of the national park – a grey area where it is easy for a corrupt official to accuse an ill-informed villager of trespassing. Illegal timber cutting is condoned, provided a fixed rate per camel cart or truck or tractor load is paid. The occasional poacher bribes his way in. The forest post is rich. The forest guard takes his cut, then passes the income up the line of authority, with each man taking a percentage until some of this illegal revenue even ends up in the cities. The system thrives on corruption and greed.

The village is at the mercy of the forest post. Its survival depends on supplies of firewood and grazing. If the villagers have to pay for access to the forest, they start to take more than they need, so that they can build up reserves; they are understandably afraid of what the future might bring – tomorrow they may be charged more money, or denied access altogether. Thus the forest is depleted. And every now and then – for the record – the guards rush in and arrest the timber merchant or the villager with his cattle. There are clashes, because the villagers have already paid their fees.

*O*utside Ranthambhore National Park after the first rains. More like a desert than a forest, it shows how urgent the need for better management of natural resources has become.

The forest post and the patrolling parties discuss the issues. More money changes hands. On the surface, everyone appears to be satisfied – but the forest is dying, the people's way of life is changing and a traditional culture is being battered beyond redemption. Occasionally, a dynamic ranger will attempt to curtail such activity, but he seldom lasts long before being transferred.

The voice from the village continues the story: 'Project Tiger was really the beginning of the end for our village. We were all compromised or turned into criminals, though some were more affected than others. Until a few years ago, we paid the forest post for our wood, grass and grazing rights. The post got richer and richer. Then greed took over when money flowed. Our forester grew greedy and in the middle of the night he persuaded many villagers to go into the forest and fill carts full of wood – not dead wood, but the wood of the precious dhok tree which we know grows so slowly. These trees were cut down for the profit that could be made from the sale of the wood. Our forest shrank.

'Somehow, with all these strange and new developments that were imposed on us without dialogue or discussion, our community feeling and the unity of the village changed. Our way of being was affected as the attraction of earning large sums of money took hold of a few. Our village has always been divided into many different communities – there are Bramahs, Baniyas, Malis, Muslims, Minas and Chamars – but whatever our religion or caste, we all had a genuine respect for the forest because of all the different ways in which it contributed to our lives.

'But this new project seems to have created a disturbance, an imbalance in our community and it has come directly from our fear of the forester and his guards, their quick abuse, their ability to register cases against us in courts whose legal processes we do not understand. Then they demand money from us, and steal the precious wood from the forest. And this corruption extends beyond the forester to the small government officials who participate in the administration of the village. Everyone

*I*nside the park during the monsoon. Lush, green and thickly forested, this remains one of the finest oases of tiger habitat. But we must work to keep it that way.

who has authority over us seems to think that this is a new way of making lots of money. In the village, this means that we have no choice but to oblige, or to turn a blind eye.'

There are other ways in which the forest officials can supplement their income. Taxi jeeps registered under assumed names and run by relatives of the officials can net a profit of 700 rupees a day – as much as a junior forest guard earns legally in a month. Entry gates find their own ways to make money from visitors, and so do forest rest houses – this money does not have to be declared to any higher authority. Some professional photographers and film-makers buy their way through the rules with gifts of cameras, film and other valuables from the West. Serious and sincere tourist management does not stand a chance.

Illegal commissions are taken from the construction of roads, dams and cattle ditches. When a cattle ditch is to be dug, fifty people may be employed for twenty days each. But if they cannot read, and understand simply that they must make a mark on a piece of paper in order to be paid, they can easily be persuaded to sign a form saying they have worked for thirty days and received thirty days' wages – in which case a substantial sum finds its way into the administrators' pockets. Only eight bags of cement are used in the construction, rather than the ten that have been allocated. Somebody will make a profit on the two missing bags, but there is also a deeper motive: sooner or later the shoddily built ditch will develop a crack and the whole operation will have to be carried out again.

The villagers have a clear idea of what is going on, but are powerless to do anything about it. Sometimes there is a complaint, which has to be seen to be investigated. But the boss does not want any controversy and certainly does not want his own compromises to be revealed. The junior officer who could be suspended for his actions knows the senior bureaucrat's son, whom he has entertained as a VIP in the park. The son exerts pressure on the father. Everything is hushed up. The park and the villagers are again the victims of a vast web of intrigue.

Perhaps the most serious issue concerns tiger poaching. In the nineteen years since Project Tiger began, at least a few tigers a year must have been killed illegally in and around Ranthambhore. But this is not just Ranthambhore's problem. It reflects what happens and has always happened throughout India's wilderness areas. The system makes it very difficult for even a committed forest officer to take action against a poacher, since if he acts he could find himself harassed by a boss who would prefer to avoid controversy. Forest officers therefore tend to toe the line and remain subservient to the system.

As far as the villagers are concerned, the first serious abuse of the forest began with the introduction of Project Tiger. The single guard who patrolled twenty kilometres of forest fringe was more honest, disciplined and hard-working than the six guards who cover the same ground today. A large amount of revenue can travel upwards, converting itself into luxurious consumer products that in turn feed the parallel economy of the private sector.

And yet there are a tiny minority of government employees who fight for their rights and work with quiet commitment. One forest guard, Badhya, who tragically died recently, symbolized the best in Ranthambhore. He had been associated with the park for sixteen years and was the silent saviour of the area, the most knowledgeable but the most humble of the guards, a master of the language of the forest. He taught me a great deal and he will be much missed.

There are others who work hard, but feel obliged to turn a blind eye to what is going on. One district officer I knew continued to fight for his principles, although he was transferred ten times in three years. It is on these people that the future depends – but they are very few.

One of the most colourful and dynamic characters in the story of Ranthambhore is Fateh Singh Rathore, who remained at the helm of Project Tiger for twelve years. Ranthambhore was his kingdom and he loved it. He was a comrade and friend to his guards and staff. His sense of the natural balance that should exist between people and forest gave him an insight into the area that no one else has had. But one man cannot protect a forest without the active support and good will of every human being that lives in and around it. Fateh Singh fought with his blood, sweat and tears, but he could not beat the system alone and he became entangled in controversies that are still with him. By the end of his time in Ranthambhore he had become more and more isolated from the system of which he was a part, and from the people and tigers he loved.

Is it any wonder that the villagers are suspicious, that they feel abused and can no longer motivate themselves to act in support of their traditional values and age-old culture? The offices in Delhi and Jaipur would rather not know what is going on, and although in the district of Sawai Madhopur everyone knows, too many people are involved – it has become the accepted norm. And this is not true only of Ranthambhore. It reflects the kind of system that has grown over the centuries and engulfs India.

Who, then, is going to give anything back to the villages? After all, it is the exploitation of their meagre resources that has made those who rule rich. Can we create a new positive energy to reduce this blatant exploitation and restore some sort of dignity? Can we learn to respect a traditional way of life and belief? Or it is too late?

A voice from the resettled village of Kailashpuri: 'We agreed to leave our traditional home in the forest for the benefit of Project Tiger. You know we were better off economically then. Each family had between thirty and sixty buffaloes. There was good grass and milk flowed like rivers in the rainy season. We prepared lots of butter and *ghee* from the milk. Our needs were simple. We lived mainly in thatched huts to protect us from the extremes of winter and summer, and from the rains. Our lives were spent exploring the forest with our buffaloes. Our children didn't need much either, not even too many clothes. There was plenty of milk and *ghee* for them to eat. They even drank milk directly from the udder of the buffalo. Their young years were spent looking after the calves. Even today, they do the same outside, although there is hardly any forest or grass around us.

'We still don't believe in a school for our children. The school never gave any interesting education, the teacher was always absent, the children learned nothing of value and there were no jobs for them when they grew up. We prefer our culture and way of life. The government does little to respect this, so we are on our own. Nobody can understand us till they go through our experience of leaving our home in order to help Project Tiger succeed. In this trauma our culture saved us.'

After the resettlement of the villages in the late 1970s, the Ranthambhore tigers were not obliged to hide so much during the day and therefore became much more visible. The whole world came to see them and clapped their hands in admiration at the success of Project Tiger. But was it success? If the villages had not been moved, the tigers would have remained nocturnal and invisible. So what? The *visibility* of tigers is not an indication of success. Nor are the so-called vast increases in tiger population in Ranthambhore. In other Project Tiger reserves there are indications that little has changed over the last twenty years – no other villages have been resettled, and the tiger population is in decline all over India.

In 1973, Ranthambhore boasted good, prime, dry, deciduous forest encompassing nearly 400 square kilometres. Today there is probably just over 300 square kilometres left. A small proportion of this toll can be attributed to the pressures of people and livestock in search of fuelwood and fodder. The rest – nearly eighty per cent – is the result of illegal felling. A villager is likely to say, 'When this project started, the forest was much better than it is today. This only confirms the project's failure.'

For the last six years, the tiger population of Ranthambhore has been virtually static – an estimated thirty-five to forty tigers, if not less, though official census figures suffer from huge margins of error. The tiger population cannot increase while the forest is shrinking. A balance has to be struck between predators and prey. Although some tigers are poached, others fight between themselves and keep the population under control. Ranthambhore is like a tiny island. Young tigers can be forced out into areas where they are vulnerable to poachers and may starve due to lack of prey.

Not one research project has been instigated by Project Tiger, Ranthambhore, in nineteen years. All the information on tiger behaviour and the changes in habits and habitat has been collected by independent initiative.

The voice from the village says, 'We live around our forest. We depend on it. Our population has increased and so has our livestock. The forest has not and will not. We know the forest has to live if we are to live. Without it we would have to leave our homes. But why, nineteen years ago, did Project Tiger waste money inside the forest and not spend it outside? After all, the gods of heaven look after the inside, giving sun and water for it to grow. What we needed was help on the outside. If we had had help then, we would have been less dependent today. The project should

A skilled painter from Sawai Madhopur shows a 'tiger's eye view' of the problems of the future, as the tigers look down on their devastated kingdom.

Community life in Lahpur, one of the villages that was resettled from inside Ranthambhore National Park in the 1970s. If the tiger survives, it will be thanks to the involvement and sacrifice of these people.

have been about the people. It could have worked on agricultural development with us. It might have saved both tiger and forest.'

Not one single alternative energy project or eco-development has been started outside the park. The district administration set up 130 biogas plants, but they are all choked up because they need to be fed at regular intervals and the cattle do not only graze near the biogas plants – their dung has to be collected from all over the forest. As things stand, it is impossible to make this enterprise viable. The villagers ask why the government wastes money on biogas when there is no cow dung: 'Why not help us with better cattle and more milk – and after that we can think of biogas. Now we are given grass for our cattle, but why has no one first improved the cattle themselves? Why does government start from the tail?'

In 1990, central government and the planning commission sanctioned an eco-development plan worth 79.2 million rupees over five years. The usual procedures followed: permission was slowly given in Delhi, then passed on to Jaipur, then eventually on to Project Tiger, Sawai Madhopur. . . .

Since the financial allocation is vast, ten senior officers in a new and supposedly dynamic administration have been appointed; their role is to ensure that the plan is implemented effectively and the delegation of responsibilities is carried out correctly.

But so far the project seems to be achieving nothing. Officers are already fighting among themselves for the spoils, and the prospect of perks and privileges has caused great divisions in the team of one hundred personnel.

Twelve million rupees are destined for livestock improvement. An excellent idea. The introduction of crossbred Jersey stud cattle would increase milk yields without reducing the native cattle's immunity to disease. The extra milk would generate income for the village and relieve pressure on the forest. But at the time of writing not a single rupee has been spent in this area.

A further 22.6 million rupees are meant for pasture development, so that the improved livestock can feed on lush green grass. Another excellent idea. But if the livestock has not been improved, it is a total waste – which is exactly what has happened. Pasture development has started before livestock improvement, and the grass is being used to feed animals that are little more than skeletons and produce no milk. But since the plan has only just started, this may be the moment to redraft it so that it becomes more viable and checks can be created to prevent its misuse. It must be based on the needs of the people.

Then there are 5.5 million rupees intended for fuelwood plantations. Not one viable attempt has been made in this direction. In other words, there has been no noticeable benefit so far from the sanctioned amount of 44.2 million rupees.

There is an allocation of 35 million rupees for equipment, construction, tourist management, civil works and establishment costs – or, to put it another way, 35 million rupees are to be spent on administering the expenditure of 44.2 million rupees. But absolutely nothing is happening in any co-ordinated way and it is frightening to think that this huge amount of money might be about to go to waste.

Our village commentator continues: 'Even when the Social Forestry Department (a sister organization of the Forestry Department whose responsibility it is to plant trees) starts by distributing trees, they grow all the wrong ones. Nobody wants them. Why don't they grow the trees of the forest? They are the best for revenue, medicine, wood and even fruit. After all, the value of this forest is that it was nature's gift, not something produced by any government. You see, government does not care. They do what they want to do. We do what we want to do. Nobody talks to us about our ideas and our ways. The forest gets smaller and smaller.

'We look at our life from day to day. We have no medical amenities, no good education for our children. The future has no hope, for what the government says it will do it never does. For us to do anything is difficult. Our resources are meagre, our traditional culture affected. But we will not bow down. One day we will fight.'

These voices reveal the severe disturbance that the villagers have suffered. In and around Ranthambhore, their way of life was closely connected to the forest and the tiger. But now man, tiger and forest are isolated from one another. If only someone had listened to these voices when Project Tiger began, and had incorporated their views into the strategies and policies for protecting the forests and the tigers, this core of opinion might have created the most dynamic plan possible for the future of the tiger, since it would have encompassed the heritage and knowledge of the people. An effective form of 'joint management' might have evolved. Or it might not. We will never know. All we can do is look at what has actually happened and see where we are stranded now.

The supposed success of the Ranthambhore Project Tiger reserve has attracted visitors from all over the world. Caring people everywhere are now aware of the tiger's problems – but the cost has run into millions and millions of rupees. The petrol bill incurred in a year by the forest department and district administration in taking VIPs around the reserve would be sufficient to sponsor a worthwhile activity in one of the villages. But do any of these people take a day off from looking for tigers in order to see the outside of the park, to sit in a village and gain some insight into the attitudes of the people? No. Nobody is really interested in the rhythms of village life. As long as the VIPs can sit in the famous forest rest house, Jogi Mahal, enjoy a free drink and a free meal and be taken round the park in a free jeep, everything is fine. In the meantime, the forests of Ranthambhore are gasping for life.

Because of the famous visibility of the tigers, Ranthambhore is like a special stage, a unique arena in which the tiger performs. But even the concerned observer who comes to watch the show is protected from the truth. Although there are nearly 300 kilometres of roads in the park, visitors are only permitted on certain specified routes, which make up less than a third of the total. They do not see the degradation of the fringe and buffer areas of the forest. These other roads are misused by tractors and camel carts for collecting large and illegal quantities of wood. If these roads were closed and wood could only be taken away by the headload, much of this despoliation would stop. Today, the children of Ranthambhore question the value of their traditional heritage. The older generation can provide few answers. The fringes of the forest, where the people live, stink of neglect. This is an example of the kind of administrative malfunctioning that has occurred over the years around Ranthambhore National Park, but such problems are a reality of life in every part of India, and even more so in the cities. They are not the fault of any individual, but of the system an individual succumbs to. The system needs attention. After decades of decay, it can only become healthy again if the people of this country strengthen themselves to prevent the exploitation they suffer.

Is there a flicker of light on the horizon? I think so. It comes from the people's resistance to change, which today as in Gandhi's time clings to the old values despite the most devastating hardships. It is this resistance which could finally keep the

*O*ne of the most fascinating features of Ranthambhore – the banyan tree. Some banyans are known to be 800 years old and are mentioned in ancient texts. Tigers use them for shelter and the future of trees and tigers are closely intertwined.

monsters of civilization away, which could germinate seeds of greenery amid the strange desert that seems to loom over the future.

There is no question of right or wrong when we consider the value of traditional patterns of life. They have to be absorbed without being judged – and that is probably more difficult for us today than it has ever been before. The only way to encourage these patterns to survive is to live with them. Throughout the world, thousands of ancient cultures have been wiped out or are in the process of vanishing. The developed world is unable to take 'folk' wisdom seriously or treat it with respect. Western scientific attitudes discard traditional ways of life and trample on them without a thought.

But the people of Ranthambhore are resisting. In the resettled complex of Kailashpuri, they hold fast to their buffaloes, their milk, their butter, their god; they consult their *bhopa* or medicine man in order to cure disease or to seek reassurance in troubled times. The *bhopa* invokes various spirits to arrive at a solution or a truth. All village decisions are taken in consultation with him. One particular cause for optimism lies in the fact that Kailashpuri has registered itself as a legal entity, a non-governmental organization which will instigate, manage and participate in its own projects. This may represent a ray of light for the tiger and his forest, as well as the people. It is all interconnected.

The tiger has had a vast effect on human life wherever it has roamed. It has been more than just a magnificent animal. It has symbolized the very essence of life and been the vital indicator of the health of a natural system. Its extinction will have far-reaching repercussions and I fear that the moment the tiger becomes extinct may represent the moment when the problems humanity faces are finally beyond solution. The finely tuned equilibrium between man and nature that flourished in the past of spiritual, cultural and natural connections will be severed and a new generation will learn to cast off the past, muddle through the present and destroy the future.

It is no longer enough to police the tiger forests of the world. Legislation to protect the forests has to be supported by the people who live in and around them. Only if this happens do the forest and its wildlife have a chance of surviving. We can no longer impose alien regulations on these people – instead we must encourage them to formulate and obey their own policies.

The fate of the 6,000 tigers remaining in the world, and their habitats, therefore rests directly with the people who live with them. If they are ignored as they have been in recent centuries, there is little hope for the survival of the tiger habitat. People must feel secure enough to participate in the protection of their forests – they must be confident that it will benefit them as well as the wildlife. They must retain a belief in the knowledge that has been handed down to them through the generations. This will nurture a sense of community and togetherness which the outside world cannot provide. If their own way of life is not under threat, they may be able to absorb some of the beneficial facets of modern thinking and technology which will enhance, support and strengthen them. In an ideal world, there would be a meeting point between traditional and modern wisdom.

This is a crucial moment in the history of the tiger. As we have seen, there are a variety of forces in play. All over the land of the tiger, the cultural fabric which wove the lives of the forest communities together has been torn apart. And as each of these cultures is endangered, so too is the tiger itself. Its survival cannot be guaranteed by Project Tiger or any other policy or plan that treats the tiger in isolation. If it does survive, it will be because the lost tribes and forest communities of the world have found a way to rise up against the holocaust they are facing in these last years of the twentieth century.

The tiger has always been the guardian and protector of the people around him; it remains to be seen whether the people can continue to be effective guardians of the tiger. There are no easy answers. The tiger's future is inextricably entangled with that of the peoples who inhabit its land. The tiger's destiny is their destiny.

A tiger walks the fringe areas of the park amid tree stumps and scenes of general degradation. This could be the image of the future unless we act to prevent it.

THE RANTHAMBHORE FOUNDATION

The Ranthambhore Foundation was born out of a passionate desire to protect our natural heritage and to secure man's place within the natural world. Experience in Ranthambhore National Park had shown that man's desperate need for survival and abuse of dwindling resources could not be separated from the protection of forests and natural areas for ecological reasons. Because man and cattle, with their endless need for pasture and the products of the forest, had created severe pressure on wilderness areas like Ranthambhore, the Foundation, in its first phases, addressed many of the problems faced by the forest communities. Centuries ago, these forest communities worshipped nature in general and the tiger in particular: both were an integral part of their culture and way of life. Today, the disruption of that way of life has done great damage to their links with the forest. The Foundation hopes to help the process that might integrate them.

The Ranthambhore Foundation was established in 1987 as a non-profit-making, non-government organization; its stated long-term objective was 'the maintenance of the essential ecological balance necessary for man to live in harmony with nature'.

Such a project could only succeed if it had the active participation and support of the villagers. One of the Foundation's primary concerns, therefore, is to involve the local communities in its work and to make them conscious of the important benefits they derive from living so close to a natural forest – a forest that runs the risk of turning into semi-desert if it is not carefully managed.

To date, the main thrust of the Foundation's activities has fallen under the following headings:

1. Health, medicine, family planning and traditional knowledge: a mobile primary health service has been implemented and has treated over 15,000 people. In addition, a recently established health service on the far side of the park will deal with 8,000–10,000 patients a year. The symbol of the health service is a tree with a family and a tiger under its canopy. Establishing a health service helped the Foundation to begin other activities.

2. Income generation in traditional skills: the revival of arts and crafts in the area has been encouraged by DASTKAR, a non-governmental organization specializing in this field. They have developed a wide range of soft furnishings and clothes using the local crafts of patchwork and embroidery, locally available block-printed and tie-dye fabrics, and traditional colours, styles and motifs. The income generated for the village is substantial (about 600,000 rupees at the time of writing) and relieves the desperation about day-to-day survival, giving people time and space to consider ecology and the environment.

The Foundation supports the Ranthambhore School of Art, where students develop skills in painting on silk, sketching and drawing. Recent successful exhibitions in Delhi and Bombay have helped generate income for the benefit of the resettled complex of Kailashpuri, as well as providing finance for the artists' future work and the training of new students. The aim here is to concentrate on themes inspired by nature, be it tiger, bird or tree, and reveal through a traditional skill the plight of man and forest.

3. Dairy development and animal husbandry: the introduction of stall-fed cattle is a vital initiative in the improvement of livestock and milk yield in the area: there are now twelve murrah buffaloes in Khilchipur village, some of the only stall-fed cattle in the area. The establishment of dairy co-operatives which sell milk to the milk union dairy is also an important step forward. Nearly 600 kilos of milk are now collected daily from five co-operatives, generating more valuable income for the villages: This venture has so far generated about 300,000 rupees for the villagers.

A programme of natural insemination and improved veterinary care for stall-fed livestock feature in the Foundation's plans for the future. Again, this activity generates vital income and the introduction of better breeds will improve milk yields and reduce livestock pressure on the forest.

4. Trees, nursery, regreening and seed collections: the Foundation's mother nursery now has a capacity of 50,000 saplings of indigenous and fruit species. From this it has established two smaller nurseries in the villages of Sherpur and Shampura, which are run by societies formed for the purpose. During 1991, 24,000 saplings were planted on protected land, in school compounds, on private land and even in the forest. The process of replanting saplings is made possible with the help of local children. Most of the schools function as plant distribution centres for the villages.

The Foundation has also established a seed bank with seeds collected from the area around the forest and stored for germination. Traditional knowledge, medicinal values and growth potentials are all studied and recorded: we glean information from the elders and the cattle grazers as well as scientists. It is only through keeping the biogenetics of the trees alive that the future of a primeval forest can be assured. Replanting trees is one of the most important areas of the Foundation's activity, aiming to create a rich and viable buffer zone between the park and the surrounding grazing land in order to stop the rapid encroachment on the forest that is currently taking place.

5. Education: At least 2000 children are involved in the Foundation's regular field trips into the park, which aim to promote environmental awareness. Other activities ranging from village plays to helping to clear rubbish from the forest are intended to increase all-round understanding of nature and the fine balance required to sustain it. The fate of the forest and the tiger will one day lie in the hands of these children. If supported and encouraged they could be the future custodians of the forest.

6. Fellowships: the first of these started in January 1992 and the Foundation intends to provide three a year for post-graduate students in various disciplines. It is hoped that their research will lead to greater knowledge of the social fabric and historical developments in the villages, in order to promote better understanding of the problems to be tackled.

7. History: At the request of the Foundation, the Indian National Trust for Art and Cultural Heritage has established a programme to restore and conserve neglected historical sites in the area.

8. Village groups: the Foundation is actively promoting the establishment of 'green groups' within the villages which will co-operate with Project Tiger in protecting forest land, starting plantations and building cattle ditches where necessary. One of the village groups is now registered as a non-governmental organization and is in a position to manage its own resources according to its own needs. This is the future. Organizations like the Ranthambhore Foundation could step back as village groups grew and strengthened.

9. Fringe area development: the Foundation has successfully liaised between village communities and the Forest Department over initiatives aimed at the protection of the forest, such as the digging of cattle ditches around the forest buffer zone and the creation of pastureland plantations in the area.

10. Water management: the Foundation has launched a comprehensive water survey with a view to organizing appropriate water management and watershed development programmes in the villages surrounding the park.

Other activities include working with the Agricultural Department to improve farming methods; promoting better land use and regreening the buffer and fringe zones of the park; retaining a lawyer to resolve some of the day-to-day problems the villagers face; maintaining a dialogue with both Project Tiger and the Forest Department; working closely with the resettled villages on a wide range of welfare schemes; investigating possible forms of alternative energy, particularly biogas using the dung of stall-fed cattle; and starting a research project on the fringe areas of the park to study tiger and leopard behaviour, their interactions with domestic livestock and their effect on crops – vital information for any long-term conservation programme.

The Ranthambhore Foundation believes that projects such as these, initiated as part of an integrated development plan and implemented with the full support and involvement of local communities, are the only way to ensure the survival of the tiger and its habitat. Ranthambhore is, at present, the only example of such a scheme. National parks like Ranthambhore are a part of the heritage of this planet. A shared concern is vital.

The Foundation's views were vitally endorsed by the Caracas Declaration of February 1992, the result of an international congress on parks, protected areas and the human future. The Declaration recognized 'that nature has intrinsic worth and warrants respect regardless of its usefulness to humanity' and 'that the future of human societies depends upon people living in peace among themselves and in harmony with nature'. It called on governments to – among other things – 'support the development of national protected area policies which are sensitive to customs and traditions, safeguard the interests of indigenous people, take full account of the roles and interests of both men and women, and respect the interests of children of this and future generations'; and 'to develop mechanisms that will allow all sectors of society, especially long-standing local populations, to be partners in the planning, establishment and management of protected areas, and will ensure they share equitably in the associated costs and benefits'.

For further information on the Ranthambhore Foundation, please contact: The Ranthambhore Foundation, 19 Kautilya Marg, Chanakyapuri, New Delhi 110 021, India or the Ranthambhore Society, Grantchester, Linden Gardens, Leatherhead, Surrey, KT22 7HB, England.

BIBLIOGRAPHY

USSR

ABRAMOV, V. K. *A contribution to the biology of the Amur tiger* Panthera tigris longipilis *(Fitzinger, 1868)* Vestnik Ceskoslovenske Spolecnosti Zoologicke 26(2): 189–202

ARAMLIEV, I. *Beyond the Ural Mountains* London 1961

ATKINSON, T. N. *Oriental and Western Siberia* 1858

—— *Travels in the Regions of the Upper and Lower Amur*, New York 1860

COXWELL, C. Fillingham (comp./ed.) *Siberian and Other Folk Tales* London 1925

DYRENKOVA, N. P. 'Bear worship among Turkish Tribes of Siberia', in *Proceedings of the Twenty-Third International Congress of Americanists*, 1928 (pp. 411–40) New York 1930

KNYSTANTAS, A. *The Natural History of the USSR* Century Hutchison, London 1987

MATJUSHKIN, E. N., SMIRNOV, E. N. and ZHYVOTCHENKO, V. I. *The Amur Tiger in the USSR*

MAZAK, V. *Notes on Siberian long-haired tiger*, Panthera tigris altaica *(Temminck, 1844), with a remark on Temminck's mammal volume of the* Fauna Japonica Mammalia 31(4): 537–73

NOVIKOV, G. *Carnivorous Mammals of the Fauna of the USSR* IPST, Washington DC 1962

OGNEV, S. *Mammals of the USSR and Adjacent Countries, III* IPST, Washington DC 1962

PRYNN, D. *Siberian Tiger Wildlife* 20(9): 398–402, 1978

ROSTOVTZEV, MICHAEL I. *The Animal Style in Southern Russia and China* Princeton 1929

SMIRNOV, E. N. *The Tiger in the USSR* IUCN, 1977

STROGANOV, S. U. *Carnivorous Mammals of Siberia* IUCN, 1969

SWAYNE, H. O. C. *Through the Highland of Siberia* London 1964

CHINA

ALLEN, G. M. *Mammals of China and Mongolia* American Museum of Natural History, New York 1938

ANDREWS, R. C. *Camps and Travels in China* London 1919

—— *Ends of the Earth* London 1929

BAIKOV, N. A. *The Manchurian Tiger* London 1925

CALDWELL, H. RUTH *Blue Tiger* London 1925

CHEN-HUANG, SHOU *Economic Animals of China* Peiping 1962

CHURCH, P. W. *Chinese Turkestan with Caravan and Rifle* London 1901

CLARKE, SAMUEL R. *Among the Tribes in South-West China* 1970

COLBERT, E. H. and HOOIJER, D. H. *Pleistocene Mammals from the Limestone Fissures of Szechwan* China Bulletin of the American Museum of Natural History 102(1): 1–134, 1935

EBERHARD, WOLFRAM *Studies in Chinese Folklore and Related Essays* Indiana University Press, Bloomington 1970

GRANET, MARCEL *Danses et Légendes de la Chine ancienne* 2 vols, Paris 1926

—— *La pensée chinoise* Paris 1934

HOOIJER, D. A. *Pleistocene Remains of* Panthera tigris *(Linnaeus) subspecies from Wanhsien, Szechan, China, compared with fossil and recent tigers from other localities*, American Museum Novitiates No. 1346, p. 17, 1947

LANNING, G. *Wildlife in China* London 1911

LATTIMORE, O. *Desert Road to Turkestan* London 1928

—— *High Tartary* Boston 1930

—— *Inner Asian Frontiers of China* New York 1940

PEI, WEN-CHUNG *On the Carnivora from locality 1 of Choukoutien* Palaeontologica Sinica, Series C, 8(1): 1–216, 1934

PREJVALSKI, N. M. *Mongolia, the Tangut Country* London 1876

QUINCY, J. W. *Chinese Hunter* London 1939

ROCK, JOSEPH *The Ancient Nakhi Kingdom of South-East China* Harvard University Press, 1947

SOWERBY, A. DE C. *The Naturalist in Manchuria* London 1928

—— *A Naturalist's Notebook in China* London 1925

—— *Sport and Science on the Sino-Mongolian Frontier* London 1918

—— *Fur and Feather in North China* Tsientsin 1914

SUTTON, J. B. *In China's Border Provinces; the turbulent career of Joseph Rock – botanist/explorer* Hastings Home

SWINHOE, R. 'On the mammals of the island of Formosa (China)' in *Proceedings of the Zoological Society* London 1862: 347–65

—— 'On the mammals of Hainan' in *Proceedings of the Zoological Society* London 1870: 224–39

WALLACE, H. F. *Big game of Central and Western China* London 1913

WERNER, CHALMERS *A Dictionary of Chinese Mythology* Kelly & Walsh, Shanghai 1932

WILLIAMS, C. A. S. *Outlines of Chinese Symbolism and Art Motives* Customs College Press, Peking 1931

YELTS, PERCEVAL *The Symbolism in Chinese Art* China Society 1912

MALAYA, INDO-CHINA AND INDONESIA

ALEXANDER, PATRICK *Spirits of the Malay Jungles* Asia, January 1935, Vol. XXXV No. 1

BORNER, M. *Status and conservation of the Sumatran Tiger* Carnivore 1(1): 97–102, 1978

BRADLEY, J. *A Narrative of Travel and Sport in Burma, Siam and the Malay Peninsula* London 1876

COLE, FAY-COOPER *The Peoples of Malaysia* New York 1945

DURAND, M. *Imagerie Populaire Vietnamienne* EFEO

EVANS, IVOR H. N. *Studies in Religion, Folklore and Custom in British North Borneo and the Malay Peninsula* Cambridge University Press, 1923

FOENANDER, E. C. *Big Game of Malaya* London 1952

HARRISON, A. *Indo-China: a Sportsman's Opportunity* Plymouth 1937

HEMMER, H. 'Fossil mammals of Java II: Zur Fossilgeschichte des Tigers (*Panthera tigris* [L.])' in *Java Proceedings of the Koninklijke Nederlandse Akademie van Wetenschappen*, Series B, 74(1): 35–52, 1971

HUBBACK, T. R. *Studies of Wildlife in a Malayan Jungle* Bombay Natural History Society

—— *Three months after Big Game in Pahang* Bombay Natural History Society

KITCHENER, H. J. *Malayan Nature Journal* 1961

MAXWELL, G. *In Malay Forests* Blackwood, London 1907

MAZAK, V. *On the Bali Tiger*, Panthera tigris balica (Schwarz 1912) Vestnik Ceskoslovenske Spolecnosti Zoologicke 40(3): 179–95, 1967

MAZAK, V; GROVES, C. P. and VAN BREE, P. J. H. 'On a skin and skull of the Bali tiger and a list of preserved specimens of *Panthera tigris balica* (Schwarz, 1912)' in *Zeitschrift fur Saugetierkunde* 43(2): 65–128, 1978

MEDWAY, Lord *The Wild Animals of Malaya* OUP, London 1969

MEYER, C. *Trapping Wild Animals in Malayan Jungles* London 1922

MONESTROL, H. de *Hunting Wild Animals of Indo-China* Saigon 1952

MONHOT, H. *Travels in Indo-China* 1864

PEACOCK, E. H. *A Game Book for Burma and Adjoining Territories* London

SKEAT, W. W. *Malay Magic* 1900

—— *Pagan Races of the Malay Peninsula* 1906

STUART-FOX, D. T. *Macan: The Balinese Tiger* Bali Post (Eng. edn.), July 23 1979 pp. 12–13

WESSING, ROBERT *The Soul of Ambiguity: the tiger in South-East Asia* Centre for South-East Asian Studies, Northern Illinois University

NEPAL, BURMA AND TIBET

BERGLIE, PER-ARNE *On the Question of Tibetan Shamanism* Zurich 1978

CORNEILLE, JEST *Tarap; one Himalayan Valley* 1974

GRAY, JAMES *Burmese Proverbs and Maxims*

GRIBBLE, R. H. *Out of the Burma Night* London 1943

HITCHCOCK, J. AND JONES, R. *Spirit Possession in the Nepal Himalayas* Warminster 1975

KINLOCH, A. A. *Large Game Shooting in Tibet and the North-West* London 1876

LIPTON, MIMI *The Tiger Rugs of Tibet* Hayward Gallery, London 1988

MORRIS, J. *Winter in Nepal* London 1963

ROERICH, J. N. *The Animal Style among the Nomad Tribes of Northern Tibet* Seminarium Kondakovianum, Prague 1930

SMYTHIES, E. A. *Big Game Shooting in Nepal* Thacker, Spink & Co, Calcutta

STAINTON, J. D. A. *Forest of Nepal* Murray, London 1972

INDIA

BALDWIN, J. *The Large and Small Game of Bengal and the North-Western Provinces of India* London 1877

BANNERJEE, S. C. *Flora and Fauna in Sanskrit Literature* Calcutta 1932

BERRIEDALE-KEITH, A. *Indian Mythology* Boston 1917

CHANDRA, SUBODH and MODE, HEINZ *Indian Folk Art*

CROOKE, WILLIAM *Religion and Folklore of Northern India* OUP, London 1926

DALMIA, Y. *The Painted World of the Warlis* Lalit Kala Academy 1988

DALTON, E. T. *Descriptive Ethnology of Bengal* Calcutta 1872

DOWSON, J. *A Classical Dictionary of Hindu Mythology* Trubner's Oriental Series, London 1879

DUTT, G. S. *The Tiger God in Bengal Art* Modern Review, Calcutta, November 1932

ELWIN, V. *The Baiga* London 1939

—— *The Muria and their Ghotul* Bombay 1947

—— *The Tribal Art of Middle India* London

ENTHOVEN *The Folklore of Bombay* Asian Education Service

FAUNTHORPE, J. C. *Jungle Life in India, Burma and Nepal* Natural History No. 2, 1924

FERNANDEZ, W., MENON, G. and VIEGAS, P. *Forests, Environment and Tribal Economy (Orissa)* Indian Social Institute

FIFE-COOKSON, COL. J. C. *Tiger shooting in the Doon and Ulwar* London 1887

FORBES *Wanderings of a Naturalist*

FORSYTH *Highlands of Central India*

GAHLOT *The Wisdom of Rajputana*

GRIERSON, G. A. *Bihar Peasant Life* Patna

GUPTA, A. 'Tigers at High Altitudes' in *Journal of the Bombay Natural History Society* 29 (1–2): 55–56, 1959

HEWETT, J. *Jungle Trails in Northern India* London 1938

HIRALAL, R. B. and RUSSELL, R. V. *The Tribes and Castes of the Central Provinces of India* London 1916

HUTTON, J. H. *The Angami Nagas* London 1921

INVERARITY, J. 'Unscientific notes on the tiger' in *Journal of the Bombay Natural History Society* 3 (3): 143–54, 1888

JULIUSSON, PER *The Gonds and their Religion* Stockholm 1974

KANHAIYALAL SAHAL *Rajasthani Kahavat Kos*

KINLOCH, A. *Large Game Shooting in Thibet, the Himalayas, Northern and Central India* Calcutta 1892

KOSAMBI, D. D. 'The Culture and Civilization of Ancient India' in *Historical Outline* No. 104 p. 89, London 1965

LEWIS, E. 'The "sambar call" of the tiger and its explanation' in the *Journal of the Bombay Natural History Society* 41(4): 889–90, 1940

LYDEKKER, R. *The Game Animals of India, Burma, Malaya and Tibet* London 1924

MAURY, CURT *Folk Origins of Indian Art* Columbia University Press, New York 1969

MILLS, J. P. *The Lotha Nagas* London 1921

—— *The Ao Nagas* London 1922

—— *The Rengma Nagas* London 1937

O'BRIEN, E. 'Where man-eating tigers occur' in *Journal of the Bombay Natural History Society* 45 (1): 231–2, 1944

O'FLAHERTY, W. D. *Sexual Metaphors and Animal Symbols in Indian Mythology* New Delhi 1980

PILGRIM, GUY E. *Fossil Carnivora of India* Calcutta 1932

POCOCK, R. 'Tigers' in *Journal of the Bombay Natural History Society* 33(3): 505–41, 1929

RISLEY, H. H. *The Tribes and Castes of Bengal* Calcutta 1891–2

RIVERS, W. H. R. *The Todas* Macmillan, London 1906

ROBERTS, T. J. *The Mammals of Pakistan* Benn, London 1977

ROWNEY, H. B. *The Wild Tribes of India* London 1882

ROY, SARAT CHANDRA *The Birhors: a little-known jungle tribe of Chota Nagpur* Ranchi, 1925

—— *The Hill Bhuiyas of Orissa* Ranchi, Man in India Office 1935

SANKALIA, H. D. *Prehistoric Art in India*

SHARMA, RAM DUTT *Sanskrit Karyon mein pasu paksi* Jaipur

SLEEMAN *Rambles and Recollections*

SMITH, W. C. *The Ao Naga Tribe of Assam* Macmillan, London

STOCKLEY, C. H. *Stalking in the Himalayas & Northern India* 1936

STUTLEY, MARGARET and JAMES *A Dictionary of Hinduism: its mythology, folklore and development* Routledge & Kegan Paul, London 1977

THURSTON, E. *Castes and Tribes of Southern India* Madras 1909

TRUMBULL *Blood Covenant*

TYLOR *Primitive Culture*

WASHBURN, H. E. *Epic Mythology* Delhi 1974

MISCELLANEOUS

ADAMS, ARTHUR *Travels of a Nauralist in Japan and Manchuria* London 1870

ARSENIEV, U. K. *Dersu the Trapper* London 1939

BALL, KATHERINE *Decorative Motives of Oriental Art* Bodley Head, London 1927

BERG, B. *Tiger und Mensch* Berlin 1934

—— *Jungle* Berlin 1935

BOHLIN, B. 'The sabre-toothed tigers once more' in *Bulletin of the Geological Institute of Uppsala* 32: 11–20, 1947

CARRUTHERS, D. *Unknown Mongolia* London 1913

—— *Beyond the Caspian* London 1949

CASSERLY, G. *In the Green Jungle* London 1927

—— *Dwellers in the Jungle* London 1925

CAVENDISH, A. E. T. *Korea and the Sacred White Mountain* London 1894

CLARKE, KENNETH *Animals and Men* Thames & Hudson, London 1977

COLLINGWOOD, C. *Rambles of a Naturalist* 1869

CUMBERLAND, C. S. *Sport on the Pamirs and Turkestan Steppes* London 1875

DASGUPTA, S. B. *Obscure Religious Cults* Calcutta 1976

DIGBY, D. *Tigers, Gold and Witchdoctors* London 1928

FISHER, J. 'Tiger! Tiger!' in *International Wildlife* 8(3): 4–11 1978

FRAZER, J. G. *Worship of Nature* London 1926

FRAZER, J. *The Golden Bough* No. 113 p. 519, Toronto 1965

HARINGTON, C. R. 'Pleistocene remains of the lion-like cat (*Panthera atrox*) from the Yukon Territory and Northern Alaska' in *Canadian Journal of Earth Sciences* 6: 1277–88, 1969

HARRINGTON, JR, FRED A. *A Guide to the Mammals of Iran* Tehran 1972

HARRISON, DAVID L. *Mammals of Arabia* Benn, London 1968

HASTINGS, J. (ed.) *Encyclopedia of Religion and Ethics* IV & V Edinburgh 1964 No. 26 p. 8

KNOWLES, G. H. *Terrors of the Jungle*, London 1932

KOCH-ISENBURG, L. *Through the Jungle Very Softly* London 1963

LAMMENS, H. *Islam: Beliefs and Institutions* Methuen 1929

LESLIE, CHARLES (ed.) *Anthropology of Folk Religion* Vintage Books New York 1960

LINDGREN, E. J. 'The Reindeer Tungus of Manchuria' in *Journal of the Royal Central Asian Society* London XXII, April 1935 pp. 221–31

LONG, REV. J. *Eastern Proverbs and Emblems* Trubner's Oriental Series, London

MALET, R. *When the Red Gods Call* London 1934

—— *Unforgiving Minutes* London 1934

MCNEELY, JEFFREY A. and WACHTEL, PAUL S. *The Soul of the Tiger* Doubleday, 1988

MITCHELL, K. W. S. *Tales from Some Eastern Jungles* London 1928

NEFF, NANCY A. *The Big Cats* Abrams, New York 1986

NYUAK, LEO 'Religious Rites and Customs of the Iban or Dyaks of Sarawak' in *Anthropos*, I pp. 11–23, 165–84, 403–25, 1906

SUTTON, R. L. *Tiger Trails in Southern Asia* London 1926

TATE, G. H. H. *Mammals of Eastern Asia* London 1947

TILSON, RONALD L. and SEAL, ULYSSES S. (eds.) *Tigers of the World* New York 1987

—— *Tiger – an Endangered Species* Noyers, New Jersey

TOYNBEE, JOCELYN *Animals in Roman Life and Art* Thames & Hudson, London 1976

TURNBULL, COLIN *The Forest People*

VAMBERY, A. *Travels in Central Asia* Murray, London 1864

VOLKER, T. *The Animal in Far Eastern Art* E. J. Brill, Leiden 1975

VOORHOEVE, R. *Harimau* London 1957

WALLIHAN, A. G. *Camera Shots at Big Game* 1901

WENSINCK, A. J. *Tree and Bird as Cosmological Symbols in Western Asia* Amsterdam 1921

WIDENGREN, GEORGE *The King and the Tree of Life in Ancient Near Eastern Religion* Uppsala 1951

WOOD, H. *The Shores of Lake Aral* London 1876

YI SANG, O. *Wild Animals of Korea* Saigon

ZOZAYONG *Korean Folk Painting* Emille Museum 1977

INDEX

PHOTO CREDITS